STANDING STRONG
in the
ANOINTING

*Discerning the Traps and
Embracing the Blessings of
Supernatural Encounters*

JAMES W. GOLL

WHITAKER
HOUSE

Unless otherwise indicated, all Scripture quotations are taken from the *New King James Version*, © 1979, 1980, 1982 by Thomas Nelson, Inc. Used by permission. All rights reserved. Scripture quotations marked (AMPC) are taken from *The Amplified® Bible, Classic Edition*, © 1954, 1958, 1962, 1964, 1965, 1987 by The Lockman Foundation. Used by permission (www.Lockman.org). All rights reserved. Scripture quotations marked (ESV) are taken from *The Holy Bible, English Standard Version*, © 2000, 2001, 1995 by Crossway Bibles, a division of Good News Publishers. Used by permission. All rights reserved. Scripture quotations marked (KJV) are taken from the King James Version of the Holy Bible. Scripture quotations marked (MEV) are taken from *The Holy Bible, Modern English Version*, © 2014 by Military Bible Association. Published and distributed by Charisma House. Scripture quotations marked (NASB) are taken from the updated *New American Standard Bible®*, © 1960, 1971, 1977, 1995, 2020 by The Lockman Foundation. Used by permission. All rights reserved. (www.Lockman.org). Scripture quotations marked (NASB95) are taken from the *New American Standard Bible®*, NASB®, © 1960, 1962, 1963, 1968, 1971, 1972, 1973, 1975, 1977, 1995 by The Lockman Foundation. Used by permission. (www.Lockman.org). Scripture quotations marked (NIV) are taken from the *Holy Bible, New International Version®*, NIV®, © 1973, 1978, 1984, 2011 by Biblica, Inc.® Used by permission. All rights reserved worldwide. The "NIV" and "New International Version" are trademarks registered in the United States Patent and Trademark Office by Biblica, Inc.® Scripture quotations marked (NLT) are taken from the *Holy Bible, New Living Translation*, © 1996, 2004, 2015 by Tyndale House Foundation. Used by permission of Tyndale House Publishers, Inc., Carol Stream, Illinois 60188. All rights reserved. Scripture quotations marked (GNT) are taken from the *Good News Translation—Second Edition*, © 1992 by the American Bible Society. Used by permission. Scripture quotations marked (TPT) are taken from *The Passion Translation,®* © 2017, 2018, 2020 by Passion & Fire Ministries, Inc. Used by permission. All rights reserved. (ThePassionTranslation.com). Boldface type in the Scripture quotations indicates the author's emphasis.

The forms L<small>ORD</small> and G<small>OD</small> (in small capital letters) in Bible quotations represent the Hebrew name for God *Yahweh* (Jehovah), while *Lord* and *God* normally represent the name *Adonai*, in accordance with the Bible version used.

S<small>TANDING</small> S<small>TRONG IN THE</small> A<small>NOINTING</small>:
Discerning the Traps and Embracing the Blessings of Supernatural Encounters

James W. Goll
God Encounters Ministries
P.O. Box 1653 • Franklin, TN 37065
www.godencounters.com • info@godencounters.com

ISBN: 979-8-88769-401-6 • eBook ISBN: 979-8-88769-402-3
Printed in the United States of America
© 2025 by James W. Goll

Whitaker House • 1030 Hunt Valley Circle • New Kensington, PA 15068
www.whitakerhouse.com

Library of Congress Control Number: 2025932258

No part of this book may be reproduced or transmitted in any form or by any means, electronic or mechanical—including photocopying, recording, or by any information storage and retrieval system—without permission in writing from the publisher. Please direct your inquiries to permissionseditor@whitakerhouse.com.

In *Standing Strong in the Anointing*, Dr. James Goll skillfully addresses a vital topic for every believer: how to navigate the powerful yet delicate realm of the anointing. With valuable insight and revelation born from his own personal encounters with the Holy Spirit and his observations of both victory and tragedy in the church, James Goll challenges us to walk in integrity while experiencing divine encounters and guarding ourselves against deception and temptation. *Standing Strong in the Anointing* offers you wisdom that will empower you to finish strong, safeguard your faith, and ensure that every supernatural experience brings you closer to the heart of Jesus. I highly recommend this timely and transformative book.

—*Patricia King*
Minister, author, media host, and producer
patriciaking.com

James Goll has been a dear friend and a prophetic voice in my life and ministry for many, many years. Whenever he releases a new book, I want to be the first to read it because I know how deeply rooted his life is in the Word of God and how attuned he is to the Holy Spirit. That makes the perfect combination for a must-read! *Standing Strong in the Anointing* is characteristically insightful, practical, and profoundly biblical. I highly recommend this book for believers of all ages and stages of life.

—*Dr. Ché Ahn*
Senior Leader, Harvest Rock Church, Pasadena, CA
President, Harvest International Ministry
International Chancellor, Wagner University

With clarity, depth, anointing, and great wisdom, this book will stir your spirit and awaken a fresh hunger for the presence and power of Holy Spirit in your life. It is not just another teaching; it is an invitation—an invitation to step into the supernatural flow of Holy Spirit's anointing while walking in the character and holiness that sustain it. The anointing is not just about power; it is about a life surrendered, yielded, and transformed in His presence. As you turn these pages, expect your heart to burn with renewed passion, your faith to rise, and your walk with the Lord to be marked by power, purity, and integrity.

—*Rebecca Greenwood*
Cofounder, Christian Harvest International and Strategic Prayer Apostolic Network
Author, *Glory Warfare* and *Discerning the Spirit Realm*

Although many preachers and teachers regularly refer to the anointing, few have found a way to describe the practical processes of maturing in the anointing, as well as avoiding the accompanying pitfalls. I am grateful to my friend James Goll for publishing a book that deals with many of the issues involved in supernatural ministry. I know this book will be a great help to thousands of believers.

—*Joan Hunter*
Author and evangelist
Host, *Miracles Happen* TV program

Walking in the glorious light of God is one of our greatest blessings in Christ. We often don't anticipate that maintaining this path could also present some of our most significant challenges as we operate in the anointing with signs and wonders and other divine supernatural manifestations. In *Standing Strong in the Anointing*, written from decades of encounters, solid biblical grounding, and fatherly love for the family of God, James Goll explains the keys to unlocking powerful supernatural experiences, as well as for operating in wisdom, boundaries, and safeguards for the anointing. Through this book, you can *walk* in God's light, *stay centered* in the light, and *continue to shine* that light as it draws people to the life-transforming love of our heavenly Father and His glory.

—*Joshua Mills*
Cofounder, International Glory Ministries
Author of many books, including *Light Warriors* and *Power Portals*

Standing Strong in the Anointing is a "now word" for the body of Christ! It may be James Goll's best book yet. James carries a unique voice of wisdom and revelation, born out of his rich personal encounters with Holy Spirit and his leadership role in several moves of God. He has experienced the anointing being manifested in and through God's people in unprecedented ways. He has also mourned as he has seen some people fall into the traps of sin and pride that destroy lives, families, and ministries. This incredible book will stir a desire in every leader and believer to demonstrate greater intimacy, power, and proficiency in the anointing of Holy Spirit, resulting in signs, wonders, miracles, and revelation for the last days' harvest. This, however, must be coupled with the character, humility, purity, and wisdom to steward their gifts in an authentic way. These pages will empower and equip believers to not only start strong but also finish well, to the glory of God.

—*Jane Hamon*
Christian International Ministries
Author, *Discernment, Declarations for Breakthrough,* and *Confronting the Thief*

Wow. What a book for our time! God is releasing a "finishing anointing" that will enable you to complete every assignment He has placed on your life. Dr. James Goll's book *Standing Strong in the Anointing* will strategically empower you to not only receive God's anointing but also sustain it for the long haul. James's wisdom will help you escape the snares the enemy would try to set for you. The anointing you develop in secret will increase your capacity to receive and sustain the external anointing God gives you for supernatural works. You will hunger for MORE of God's presence and power and will experience the anointing in new, tangible ways. Get ready to be accelerated into new divine encounters, graces, and mantles as the Holy Spirit ministers to you through these pages. This book is for everyone who loves the Holy Spirit and desires to see His presence overflow from their life.

—*Matt Sorger*
Prophetic minister, TV host, and mentor
Founder, Matt Sorger Ministries and Rescue1
Author, *God's Unstoppable Breakthrough*

DEDICATION

Over the decades, I have participated in different movements of the Holy Spirit and gleaned a depth of understanding from a variety of leaders in the body of Christ. I have made it my aim to be one who walks in the Acts 13 model of the school of the Word and the school of the Spirit brought together.

With this in mind, I wish to dedicate *Standing Strong in the Anointing: Discerning the Traps and Embracing the Blessings of Supernatural Encounters* to the teachers who taught me, the pastors who loved me, the prophets who guided me, the apostles who supplied structure, and the evangelists who brought the good news. Thank You, Holy Spirit, for giving men and women as gifts.

May this book be a tool that will help people be grounded in the Word, the will, and the ways of God and supply guardrails so they will stay the course and finish well.

CONTENTS

Foreword by Kris Vallotton 9

Acknowledgments 11

Introduction: Observing the Ways of God with Man 13

PART ONE: UNDERSTANDING THE ANOINTING

1. The Supernatural Anointing 19
2. Releasing the Supernatural Activity of the Spirit 27
3. Cooperating with the Anointing 39
4. Deceived While Yet Anointed? 57
5. Protecting the Anointing 71

PART TWO: INTERPRETING THE WAYS OF THE SPIRIT

6. The Diversity of Supernatural Encounters 85

7. Understanding Prophetic Actions 103

8. Keys to Unlocking Supernatural Encounters 115

9. Your Invitation to God Encounters 129

PART THREE: WALKING WISELY IN DIVINE ENCOUNTERS

10. Handling Complex Supernatural Experiences 145

11. Wisdom, Boundaries, and Safeguards for Your Journey 159

12. The Goal of Supernatural Encounters: Revealing Jesus 177

About the Author 191

FOREWORD

I propose that we are living in an era when the spiritual atmosphere is charged with both promise and peril. The world is crying out for the supernatural, yet many people have been ensnared by counterfeit encounters that lead them further from the truth instead of drawing them deeper into God's presence. It is incumbent upon us—especially those who walk in the prophetic, healing, and deliverance movements—to discern the difference between divine encounters that lead to transformation and deceptive experiences that can lead to destruction.

I have known James W. Goll for years, and if there's anyone who embodies both the power of the anointing and the wisdom to steward it well, it is he. James is not just a prophetic pioneer; he is a seasoned father in the faith, carrying the scars and victories of decades spent in the presence of God. What I love about James is that he doesn't just teach from theory—he shares from real-life encounters, mistakes, and hard-won wisdom that keep us anchored in the truth while embracing the power of the Holy Spirit.

This book, *Standing Strong in the Anointing*, is a crucial guide for every believer who desires to understand the anointing, interpret the ways of the Spirit, and walk wisely in divine encounters without losing their footing. With remarkable insight, James lays out the principles for discerning the authenticity of supernatural encounters, protecting the anointing on our lives, and partnering with the Holy Spirit to fulfill our divine assignments.

Let me be clear: the anointing is not a free pass to do whatever we want. It is a sacred trust, a divine enablement that must be stewarded with both humility and reverence. As James reminds us, history is filled with those who started strong in the Spirit but lost their way because they neglected the safeguards of character, community, and accountability. We cannot afford to make the same mistakes. That's why I believe this book is so timely.

Standing Strong in the Anointing is not just for experiencing the supernatural but for living in a way that ensures we will still be standing strong decades from now. Whether you are a seasoned leader or are just beginning to step into the anointing, this book will equip you to walk in power while remaining deeply rooted in Christ.

Did you catch that? The goal is not just to start well but to finish well. My prayer is that, as you read this book, you will be empowered to run your race with endurance, discern the traps of the enemy, and embrace the blessings of true supernatural encounters with God. It's time that we, as the body of Christ, stepped into the fullness of all that is available to us as believers—strong, unwavering, and anointed.

Lean in. Read with an open heart. And may you stand strong in the anointing.

—Kris Vallotton
Senior Associate Leader of Bethel Church, Redding, California
Cofounder of Bethel School of Supernatural Ministry
Author of several books, including *Uprising* and *Deliver Us from Evil*

ACKNOWLEDGMENTS

Every book is always a team effort. The older I get, the more aware I am of this reality. I am a very limited man. God gives grace to the weak, and some of that grace is manifested in and through other people that God has put around me. This book has taken years to compose. It started out as a detailed class called "Understanding Supernatural Encounters," which I taught after I moved from Kansas City to Nashville. That became one of many study guides with a grey cover and black ink, accompanied by about sixteen scratchy audiocassette tape messages.

So, where do I begin to give acknowledgments? Let's start with the many different board and staff members of Ministry to the Nations, which emerged as God Encounters Ministries (GEM). I want to give a special thank-you to Kay Durham Fee, who has served this ministry for many years. She first assisted Michal Ann, and she has been my financial administrator for years now and continues to serve in this way. Thank you for holding up my hands.

I cannot begin to express how deeply grateful I am to all those who have such a heart of devotion to the Lord Jesus Christ and have given many hours of perseverance and faithfulness to myself and GEM.

Thank you to each and every one.

INTRODUCTION: OBSERVING THE WAYS OF GOD WITH MAN

I now look through a lens of fifty years of full-time vocational ministry. During that tenure, I've had the privilege to walk alongside many men and women who appear from the stage—and even in close relationship—to be very godly. They have demonstrated signs and wonders and have brought great glory to Jesus. Some have remained strong in the power of the Spirit and the fruit of the Spirit. I have observed others who have not just fallen into various levels of sin but have continued in it, bringing disgrace to their names, their families, their ministries, and the body of Christ as a whole.

It is easier than some might think to start out hot but become lukewarm, to hate sin but then begin to tolerate it, and to do many good deeds in Jesus's name but then fall into immorality. Jesus spoke to these issues in His revelation to John. Chapters 2–3 of the book of Revelation document seven times when Jesus warned the churches, in effect, "Anyone with ears to hear must listen to the Spirit and understand what

He is saying to the churches." Jesus is very interested in how we use His power and represent His name.

I've written this book because I've seen and experienced both the traps and the blessings related to the anointing. Regularly, we see reports in the media of the moral failure of Christians. What we don't see as often—though they still occur—are the glorious miracles performed by faithful Jesus-followers around the world who are walking humbly yet powerfully in the anointing of the Spirit. God is truly working today! But how can we be among those who discern the traps of the enemy, embrace the blessings of supernatural encounters with God, and remain centered and grounded in Christ? That is what this double-edged book is about.

As a father in the faith of the global prayer and prophetic movements, I am eager to share these lessons to help you understand the anointing of the Holy Spirit, interpret the supernatural encounters that often accompany it, and walk in the wisdom of the Spirit so you can stand strong in the anointing today and not become a casualty tomorrow.

At the end of his life, the apostle Paul wrote these words in 2 Timothy 4:7–8 (NIV):

> *I have fought the good fight, I have finished the race, I have kept the faith. Now there is in store for me the crown of righteousness, which the Lord, the righteous Judge, will award to me on that day—and not only to me, but also to all who have longed for his appearing.*

This is my prayer for you, whether you are just beginning to learn about the anointing or you have been stewarding the power of God faithfully for years. I want you to be able to say that you have fought the good fight, you have finished the race, and you have kept the faith. There is most certainly a crown of righteousness waiting for each of us. Yet because we have an enemy *"seeking whom he may devour"* (1 Peter 5:8), we need the wisdom of the Spirit more than ever so we can stand strong in the anointing of Jesus.

I invite you to pray with me as we begin this book together:

Father God, thank You for the opportunity to lean into Your heart and into Your Word. I ask for Your supernatural enablement of grace to be able to learn of You and to go further, higher, wider, and deeper into Your love and into the realms that You desire for me in my life. I'm grateful for equippers in the body of Christ, and I'm thankful that You said to come and learn from You. That's what I'm planning to do, in the mighty name of Jesus. Amen and amen!

… PART ONE

UNDERSTANDING THE ANOINTING

1

THE SUPERNATURAL ANOINTING

*"The Spirit of the LORD is upon Me, because He has anointed
Me to preach the gospel to the poor; He has sent Me to heal
the brokenhearted, to proclaim liberty to the captives and recovery
of sight to the blind, to set at liberty those who are oppressed;
to proclaim the acceptable year of the LORD."*
—Luke 4:18–19

When people say, "Wow, I can feel the anointing," what are they feeling? Possibly they are getting goose bumps on their arms, or tears are welling up in their eyes as a response. Or what does it really mean when someone expresses, "That sermon was so anointed"? That statement usually implies that a person was experiencing more than just words coming from the speaker. Maybe they felt a weightiness resulting in a lingering effect of the stunning words they heard. Or perhaps someone says, "I just love getting under their anointing." Often, people go to specific ministries or events hoping that, by being around their favorite leader, they will receive a special grace to meet the felt desires or needs they have at that point in time.

The supernatural anointing makes all the difference! What is the X factor? Or is it *who* is the X factor? There is a distinction between achieving excellence in the natural realm and experiencing the brilliance of God's great presence—and the latter comes only when we are touched by God's anointing. Do you want your generation to be impressed by your great talent, or do you want to leave people with the lingering supernatural presence that comes from your spending time with the great Someone?

DEFINING THE ANOINTING

So, what is the anointing? Here is my definition: the anointing is the presence and the power of God made manifest as it comes upon consecrated ones of the Lord. That's a loaded sentence! Let's break it down into four short phrases:

- The presence and the power of God (the empowering of the Holy Spirit)
- Made manifest (becoming apparent or evident in a situation)
- As it comes upon (as God places it upon)
- Consecrated ones of the Lord (those who are set apart for the Lord for a specific service)

As noted above, consecrated ones are those who are set apart specifically for God. We can consecrate ourselves—in other words, set ourselves apart to be available to the Lord for His supernatural enablement. Or consecration may originate with the Lord as He takes the initiative to set apart someone or something for Himself, His distinct calling, or

His divine purpose. (See Acts 13:1–3 for an example of specific disciples being set apart for a distinct purpose.)

The anointing is also the power and the presence of the Holy Spirit that comes upon a person, attesting to the work of consecration in their life. We have no better example of what the anointing is and does than the life of Jesus, the Anointed One. Acts 10:38 says that *"God anointed Jesus of Nazareth with the Holy Spirit and with power, who went about doing good and healing all who were oppressed by the devil, for God was with Him."*

Thus, the presence of the anointing (with accompanying manifestations of the power of God) or the absence of the anointing (with demonstrations of human ability alone) makes all the difference in the world to our effectiveness for God. In the same way that He anointed Jesus, God wants to anoint us so we can be effective workers in His kingdom. *Without* the anointing of God, we are left to the best we can do on our own. Who wants that? But *with* the anointing of God, all things are possible. (See, for example, Matthew 19:26.)

Let me now weave in some narrative that comes from my own storyline.

TWO DROPS OF THE ANOINTING

In 1983, I was pastoring at Harvest Fellowship in Warrensburg, Missouri. At that time, I did a lot of individual counseling in my pastoral ministry. In July of that year, I attended a Kenneth Hagin camp meeting in Tulsa, Oklahoma. While I was in worship, the voice of the Holy Spirit came to me and said, "Five minutes of My anointed prayer through you will do more than five hours of the counseling you have done in the past."

My logical mind analyzed that statement and thought, "I sure could use the extra four hours and fifty-five minutes." This is not to say that my counseling had no value. The Lord was simply presenting a principle to me. He was saying that only a few minutes of His supernaturally anointed prayer through me could have an effect far beyond what my human intellect, training, or counseling skills could ever do.

When the Holy Spirit began to teach me about the anointing, I felt liberated to realize that the Holy Spirit wanted to help me, my schedule, and the people He would bring into my life. He knew that I loved to pray, and He was trying to show me that I could turn my vertical connection to Him into anointed prayer for others for supernatural impact.

This was one of the most defining words of my life, and, the following year, I had one of the most defining supernatural encounters of my life. I had planned to go to Oklahoma for another camp meeting, but the Holy Spirit spoke to me and told me not to attend. Instead, the associate pastor and his wife were to go, and I was to stay home but keep my schedule free. God's direction was clear: the time I would have spent away at the conference, I was to invest in praying and seeking Him.

On one of those days, I chose to go to a small prayer chapel on the nearby university campus—a place where I frequently had met with the Lord during the Jesus People Movement years earlier. I approached one of the pews, lowered the kneeler connected to the back of the pew in front of me, and took my place to pray. As my head was bowed, I felt someone enter the small, intimate room. Then I perceived that Someone had, indeed, entered the room as the Holy Spirit began to speak to me. He gave some very detailed directives—certain things that were very personal, and other things that He wanted me to accomplish quickly, wisely, and correctly.

Then the conversation shifted, and the Holy Spirit said to me, "Stand up." My reasoner kicked in gear and started to debate what I was hearing. Then I thought, "What difference does it make? There's no one around." So I stood up.

I still had my eyes closed, and He said, "Step out into the aisle." I stepped out into the aisle. Then He said, "Step forward."

"Huh?" I wondered. But I stepped forward.

He repeated, "Step forward." I stepped forward again, taking little baby steps. He said again, "Step forward." I had a strong awareness of the fear of the Lord, and He said to me yet again, "Step forward."

I finally opened my eyes, and, in a visionary experience, I saw myself face-to-face with Jesus, my Lord. Then He said one more time, "Step forward." As I took one more six-inch step, it seemed as if I stepped into Him and He stepped into me. At that point, Jesus was no longer externally visible; He was now vibrating within me!

I then found myself on my knees in worship. The voice of the Holy Spirit said, "I am now giving you two drops of My golden anointing." In the Spirit, in an open vision, I saw a golden pitcher positioned above my head, and, in utter amazement, I watched it tip. I felt one, then two, drops of what was like golden honey fall right smack-dab upon the top of my head. It was the golden anointing. The voice of the Lord continued, "One drop is for you, and the other drop you are to give to your wife. But a time will come in the future when I will pour the golden anointing upon your head."

I remained in reverent worship—in prayer and weeping. Then, the manifest presence of God began to lift, and I went home. I didn't tell my wife about this occurrence for a while. I wasn't sure what to do with what I had seen and heard. Later, she asked me about my time at the prayer chapel. I told her the story, smiled, and then obediently and in faith anointed her with one drop of oil. Little did I know that, a decade or so later, God would come to visit our house for nine straight weeks to fulfill His promise to pour out upon us the fullness of His golden anointing. Consider this, as well: Years later, we were both consecrated as prophets unto the Lord by Ché Ahn, Lou Engle, and others as a part of the emerging Harvest International Ministry (HIM) apostolic team. When they prayed for us, they poured oil upon our heads, and we were drenched in a golden oil that flowed from our heads to the floor. What I know is this: if you are faithful with one drop of His golden anointing, you will receive more!

While this is a very personal story, I share it with you because I want you to have faith for your own supernatural encounters with God, which will release His precious, lingering anointing upon your life. Jesus desires to be one with you and to anoint *you* for His kingdom work also.

WHEN GOD TOUCHES YOU

In July 1991, a clear prophetic word to the church came from Rodney Howard-Browne, a revivalist from South Africa who became a missionary to the United States of America. He declared:

> The great men and women of God that I am using in the earth today are not being used because they are something special. I am using them for one reason and one reason alone. It's because they've touched Me and I have touched them.[1]

Let that sink in. The anointing of the Spirit comes from a supernatural encounter with Jesus as you touch Him, and He touches you. When Jesus, the Anointed One, touches you, you will see His anointed work in your life to do what He did. In the same way that the Spirit of the Lord anointed Jesus, He wants to anoint you. What will be the result of that supernatural encounter? Luke 4:18–19 explains: *"To preach the gospel to the poor;…to heal the brokenhearted, to proclaim liberty to the captives and recovery of sight to the blind, to set at liberty those who are oppressed; to proclaim the acceptable year of the LORD."*

---

1. Rodney M. Howard-Browne, *The Touch of God: A Practical Handbook on the Anointing* (Tampa: Revival Ministries International, 1992), vi.

PRAYER TO RECEIVE THE SUPERNATURAL ANOINTING

Yes, Lord, encounter me and anoint me with the oil of Your presence, for Your glory! Fill me afresh with the Holy Spirit and let Your anointing overflow to others. I long to see power encounters, healing encounters—supernatural encounters of every biblical type—happen through me, around me, and in spite of me, for Jesus Christ's sake! I want to be a faithful steward with every drop of the anointing You grant me. Come, Holy Spirit, come! Amen and amen!

RELEASING THE SUPERNATURAL ACTIVITY OF THE SPIRIT

"The L ORD doesn't see things the way you see them. People judge by outward appearance, but the L ORD looks at the heart."
—1 Samuel 16:7 (NLT)

A. W. Tozer is credited as saying, "If the Holy Spirit was withdrawn from the church today, 95 percent of what we do would go on and no one would know the difference. If the Holy Spirit had been withdrawn from the New Testament church, 95 percent of what they did would stop, and everybody would know the difference."[2]

We need the movement and the activity of the Holy Spirit! We are dependent upon Him to produce abundant spiritual fruit. The list of exceptional human achievements throughout history is long. It's easy to be temporarily enamored of our own accomplishments. But what God

---
2. A. W. Tozer, "Quotes—Quotable Quote," Goodreads, https://www.goodreads.com/quotes/964813-if-the-holy-spirit-was-withdrawn-from-the-church-today.

can do exceeds them all! This is why we are so interested in the supernatural. Because the natural isn't super enough!

It is we, the anointed followers of Jesus, who have been entrusted with the supernatural power and presence of God. So, what are the trigger points that need to be activated so that the supernatural dimension is comingled with the natural realm? Over the years, I've observed three key elements that release the supernatural activity of the Holy Spirit: (1) the faith of God, (2) the presence of God made manifest, and (3) gifted imparters—people who release the power of God's presence to others. Let's look at each of these aspects, along with some examples from church history and my own life and ministry.

1. THE FAITH OF GOD

Faith is the first key element that is required to experience the supernatural activity of the Holy Spirit. If it's not your own faith, then it's someone else's faith on your behalf. There are three main categories of faith I'd like to highlight briefly.

First, Romans 12:3–8 teaches that *"God has dealt to each one a measure of faith"* (verse 3), and He wants each born-again believer to use this *"measure of faith"* according to the grace they have been given. Just as we must work out our physical muscles for them to grow, we must work out our measure of faith for it to increase. That's why you'll see some people operating at a higher level of faith than others.

We see a second category of faith within the fruit of the Spirit described in Galatians 5:22–23: being full of faith, or faithful. Faithfulness is one of God's immutable qualities and one He builds into the character of a believer through the Holy Spirit.

Lastly, there is the "gift of faith," which is a special surge of confidence in God and His Word that sometimes arises within a person when they face a specific situation or need. Jesus said that faith in

God is what moves mountains and answers prayers. (See, for example, Mark 11:22–24.) Have you realized that the kingdom of God is a speech-activated kingdom? Faith speaks! One important interpretation of this passage in Mark 11 involves a key phrase where Jesus indicates "Have God's faith," not just "Have faith in God." This is where the gift of faith comes in. The "gift of faith" is a portion of God's supernatural faith. Sounds good to me!

How does this faith come? Romans 10:17 instructs us that faith comes and continues to come by the *rhema* (spoken) words of Christ. There are two ways of exercising this kind of faith: to speak to God *on behalf of a person, object, or situation*; and to speak to a person, object, or situation *on behalf of God*. As we grow in our understanding and our faith, we see supernatural activity in these ways.

For example, in 1 Kings 17:1, we see how the words of the prophet Elijah controlled the dew and the rainfall. Elijah spoke, and it stopped raining. When it was time for rain again, Elijah spoke to God on behalf of the rain, and the rain fell. (Note how James 5:16–18 fills in the details of the account in 1 Kings 18:41–45.) But do I think that all this occurred by Elijah's command? No, Elijah spoke from his relationship with God. I especially love how James 5:17 says that *"Elijah was a man with a nature like ours,"* showing us that even though we are weak like Elijah, we, too, can pray, and God will do mighty things.

We can become quite comfortable talking to God about people and situations. But what happens when God leads us to speak to a person, object, or situation on His behalf? When the Israelites were in the middle of defeating their enemies, Joshua spoke to the sun and moon to stand still on behalf of God (see Joshua 10:12–14), and the sun and moon obeyed!

How is this kind of faith built? Such faith is built in us as we hear and do the Word of God. Let's not harden our hearts when we hear the Lord's voice. Instead, let's release our faith toward and in God, and anticipate great things! I'll never forget hearing Derek Prince say, "All progress in the Christian life is by faith."[3] This is why faith is so necessary.

2. THE PRESENCE OF GOD MADE MANIFEST

A second key for releasing the supernatural activity of the Spirit is the presence of God made manifest—when the power of the Holy Spirit is released at a specific time and setting. Luke 5:17 (NASB) says, *"And the power of the Lord was present for [Jesus] to perform healing."* God's power was what? It was *present*. Wouldn't the power of the Lord be present if Jesus was present? Not necessarily. The Bible shows us that Jesus relied on the anointing of the Holy Spirit in the same way we have to rely on the Holy Spirit. First, we must have faith, and then we must look for the manifest, tangible presence of God to come on the scene to enable us for action.

We can see this pattern in Mark 5:21–34. A woman with a hemorrhage of blood reached out to Jesus in desperation and expectation as He was passing by. Verse 30 (NASB95) says that Jesus *"perceiv[ed] in Himself that the power proceeding from Him had gone forth."* There was power proceeding from Him. This was the anointing of the Spirit flowing through Jesus.

In the Old Testament, we see the sovereign power of the Lord's presence on a geographical region or even on material things. This power brings an increase in the strength of the anointing. For example, 2 Kings 13:20–21 records an incident in which a man's dead body was thrown upon the dead bones of Elisha. Dead plus dead equals dead, right? No! The power of God remained upon Elisha's bones so that the man came to life as he touched them. In the New Testament, we see how *"extraordinary miracles"* of healing and deliverance happened as people carried handkerchiefs and aprons from Paul's body to the sick.

---

3. This statement may also be found in Derek Prince, *God's Word Heals* (New Kensington, PA: Whitaker House, 2010), 114.

(See Acts 19:11–12, various translations.) These articles appeared to carry a residue of the manifest power and presence of God.

In the last chapter of my book *The Seer*, I wrote about the "open heavens" that historically occurred over the Hebrides islands off the west coast of Scotland from 1949–1953. The behind-the-scenes intercession of two consecrated and anointed sisters in their eighties, Peggy and Christine Smith, released a heavy anointing upon Duncan Campbell, who was called to be the steward of the revival. An actual, tangible geographical sphere of God's presence saturated with the Spirit of conviction occurred within a five-mile radius. Whoever stepped into that zone would come under conviction of sin and cry out to God to be saved! God wants to release His supernatural presence once again in specific geographical areas for His divine purposes today!

3. GIFTED IMPARTERS

Gifted imparters are a third key element that releases the supernatural activity of the Holy Spirit. Imparters are anointed people who can transfer the power and the presence of God to others. Are there any imparters in the Bible? Yes! Let's begin with the example of the apostle Paul, who longed to see the believers in Rome so he could *"impart to [them] some spiritual gift, so that [they] may be established"* (Romans 1:11).

We find precedent for "impartation" in Numbers 27:18–23, when Moses chose his successor. Joshua had served under Moses for many years. Then there came a time when the Lord instructed Moses to publicly lay his hands upon this next-generation leader and transfer some of his authority and power to him. Deuteronomy 34:9 verifies that the impartation had an effect: *"the children of Israel heeded him."*

We can also learn from the relationship between Elijah and Elisha. (See 1 Kings 19:15–21; 2 Kings 2:1–14.) This example requires wise application. You can't just grab hold of someone's anointed mantle and "get it." There were years in which Elisha was mentored by Elijah, in which he served and learned, and this allowed Elisha to come into a supernatural realm where there was a double portion of anointing.

Last, I'll mention King Saul, who was changed into another man as he came into the prophetic presence and influence of God that was upon others. (See 1 Samuel 10:5–12; 19:20–24.)

These are a few examples of imparters in the Bible, and I'll also share briefly concerning two imparters whom I have known personally: Jill Austin of Master Potter Ministries and Bishop Bill Hamon, founder of Christian International Ministries and a modern father of the global prophetic movement.

Jill went to be with the Lord in January 2009, four months after my wife, Michal Ann, departed to her heavenly reward. The world was so greatly impacted by this prophetic imparter of the Holy Spirit. I knew no one who moved in the raw impartation of the power of God, the supernatural realm of the Holy Spirit, and the fire of God like she did. Bishop Bill Hamon has imparted or activated the gift of prophecy to more people than anyone, I believe, in modern church history. I just had the honor of giving a presentation at the celebration of his ninetieth birthday and seventieth anniversary in full-time vocational ministry. Bishop Hamon is a legend in our own time, combining character, charisma, and truth.

IMPORTANT INGREDIENTS FOR MOVING IN THE SUPERNATURAL

There are three more essential ingredients we must embrace in order to move in the powerful, supernatural presence of God: *compassion, the will and Word of God,* and *the proper timing of a matter.* Let's look briefly at each of these ingredients.

Compassion. Just before my wife, Michal Ann, went to be with the Lord, I was ministering at a conference hosted by my dear friends

Mahesh and Bonnie Chavda. Seer-prophet Bob Jones lived nearby, and he and I had the opportunity to share an afternoon together. At one point during our conversation, he looked at me and said, "Well, you've got revelation down, but your next assignment is compassion." This word had layers of meaning for me. Michal Ann had started a ministry called Compassion Acts. I also knew that Bob was showing me that an essential ingredient for moving in the powerful supernatural presence of God is to have a heart of compassion. Jesus's miraculous acts, along with the people around Him knowing they were truly valued and loved by God, came about because Jesus walked in compassion. When compassion erupts, supernatural realms open.[4]

The will and the word of God. The will of God is in the Word of God, and both are paramount in all activity of the Spirit. We must become convinced of the will of God in a specific matter to be empowered to exercise true biblical faith. Romans 12:2 instructs us to renew our minds—with the Word of God, of course—so that we *"may prove what is that good and acceptable and perfect will of God."* First John 5:15 (NASB) reads, *"If we know that He hears us in whatever we ask, we know that we have the requests which we have asked from Him."* We don't just "wish upon a star" and hope for the best. We learn the will of God from the Word of God so we can pray the will of God.

The timing of a matter. The timing of the activity of the Spirit can be mysterious. When does God want a supernatural act demonstrated, and why does He want it demonstrated? There are two Greek words for "time": *chronos* and *kairos*. *Chronos* refers to time in sequence or season, whereas *kairos* is all about the right or strategic moment. We must seek the strategic timing of God in a matter. As humans, we want the superhero to come in and save the day as soon as things start to look bleak. But God may allow us to dangle while waiting for His timing to

---

4. For more on this subject, see chapter 3, "Jesus and the Heart of Compassion," in my book *The Feeler*. (There is also an online class with a curriculum kit under the same title.)

click into place. God is as interested in the process of our becoming like Christ as He is in our receiving the promises of Christ.

Yes, Lord, fill me with all I need at the right time to see the anointed, supernatural activity of the Spirit in my life.

STEPS TO RELEASING THE ANOINTING

I have learned that there are three main steps to releasing the anointing of the Spirit: (1) look deeper, (2) look longer, and (3) worship while you wait. Three prophetic characters in Scripture provide helpful lessons on these steps to releasing the anointing in order to encounter the supernatural: Samuel, Simeon, and David.

1. LOOK DEEPER

The story of how Samuel anointed the second king of Israel provides an insightful look at how the supernatural anointing works in our lives today. After God rejected Saul as king of Israel, He told the prophet Samuel to fill his flask with oil, go to Bethlehem, and find the next king from among the sons of a man named Jesse. (Read 1 Samuel 16:1–13 for the full story.)

Samuel arrives, and Jesse has gathered seven of his sons. What does Samuel do? He looks at Jesse's first son and thinks, *"Surely this is the* Lord's *anointed!"* (verse 6 NLT). He gets out the oil and is about to pour it on the firstborn. That's the obvious choice!

But then the Holy Spirit's internal check seems to go against the Jewish principle of anointing the firstborn son. At that moment, God makes a remarkable statement: *"Don't judge by his appearance or height, for I have rejected him. The* Lord *doesn't see things the way you see them. People judge by outward appearance, but the* Lord *looks at the heart"* (verse 7 NLT). This shows us how, at times, in strategic decision-making situations, we need to pray through all the options present and not judge by what we can see, even if we have a track record of success.

Jesse then continues to have each of his sons pass before Samuel, but the Lord does not indicate to Samuel that any of them is the one He has chosen. Samuel asks Jesse if he has any more sons. Jesse replies, "Yeah, I've got one more. He's kind of…I don't know, the artsy kid. He's out in the fields with the sheep and goats, playing his harp." (See verse 11.) When David arrives, the Lord says to Samuel, *"This is the one; anoint him"* (verse 12 NLT).

When you have been anointed by God for the supernatural, you must go out in faith and obedience with what you know and have received from the Lord. Samuel received his instructions from the Lord, and he obeyed. He had thought it was an open-and-shut assignment of "anoint the firstborn son to be the next king." While the situation played out differently than Samuel had anticipated, God stepped in to teach Samuel a lesson that still resounds today: *Look deeper than what you can see in the natural.* Samuel clicked into another gear to step out with what the Lord had given to him, and then he patiently discerned whom God was anointing to be the next and most beloved king in Israel's history. We, too, can strike the mark as we follow the Holy Spirit and stand strong in His anointing.

2. LOOK LONGER

Luke 2:25–26 (NLT) shares the account of Simeon, who *"was righteous and devout and was eagerly waiting for the Messiah to come and rescue Israel. The Holy Spirit was upon him and had revealed to him that he would not die until he had seen the Lord's Messiah."*

This elderly man teaches us the lesson to never *stop* looking. Simeon had waited and waited. He shows us how important it is to continue to look until our eyes light upon what or whom the Lord has chosen. Let us pray for the eyes of Simeon so that we can receive a promise, continue to be patient for its fulfillment, watch and pray, and then be part of the work of the Spirit when the time is right.

3. WORSHIP WHILE YOU WAIT

Again, looking deeper and longer requires patience. What should you do as you wait upon the Lord, even for decades, for God's promises to come to pass? Worship! Worship while you wait. The ability to wait and remain connected to Jesus through worship is a critical element of releasing the anointing. We attract the presence of the Spirit as we manifest the godly attribute of patience. Hear what the Holy Spirit spoke to the seer-prophet John Paul Jackson, a dear friend of mine who has graduated to be with our Lord Jesus: "Tell them if they'll wait, I will come."

Worship was the attitude and posture of many who came to Jesus for a supernatural touch. They would bow in reverence and worship before they made their request. (See, for example, Luke 5:12; 8:41–42.) Do you know how long David had to wait from the time he was anointed as king by Samuel to the time he was king over all of Israel? Fifteen to twenty years! What did David do during that time? He obeyed, praised, and worshipped God. Much of the book of Psalms is the result of David's praise and worship as he waited on the Lord to come through on his behalf in a way only God could. How many anointed songs have been written from David's words? The anointing is released as we learn to wait patiently and worshipfully.

THERE ARE NO SHORTCUTS

In chapter 1, I defined the anointing as the presence and the power of God made manifest as it comes upon consecrated ones of the Lord. What a privilege it is to be entrusted by God to demonstrate the power of the gospel through signs and wonders. But the enemy will tempt us to take shortcuts to the anointing. These shortcuts weaken our ability to stand strong so we can experience the blessing of God's presence.

I hope you can see that it takes more than a prayer of impartation or a supernatural encounter to walk in the power of the Spirit. We need a touch of God upon our lives, but then we must step into Jesus with our faith and encounter His presence. We must receive Jesus's heart of compassion and store up the Word of God in our hearts so we can pray the will of God. The ability to be patient over time is also necessary, looking deeper and longer to see what God wants to do so we can follow His lead.

I've seen too many anointed people fall, and I don't want that to happen to you. So, while I will encourage you to pursue the supernatural manifestations that come through the anointing, the purpose of this book is also to provide you with understanding and wisdom about the supernatural ways of God so you can go the distance. I want you to hear from Jesus, "Well done, good and faithful servant." (See, for example, Matthew 25:21.) We need the anointing for effective work, and we must also choose to handle the power and presence of God with wisdom in the fear of the Lord. Let's grow up so we don't blow up!

PRAYER TO GROW IN THE SUPERNATURAL

Heavenly Father, in the precious name of the Lord Jesus Christ, I want to grow in the supernatural anointing of the Holy Spirit. I desire to grow in the compassion of Christ, have the eyes of Simeon, and know how to discern Your timing. I commit myself to be a person who uses the measure of faith You have given to me to operate in the gifts of the Spirit to a greater degree. Send imparters and fire-starters into my life as I consecrate myself to become an imparter to others. I declare that I will give away what has been given to me! I believe that something supernatural is just about to happen in and through my life, for such a time as this, for the glory of God. Amen and amen!

3

COOPERATING WITH THE ANOINTING

"And when they had prayed, the place where they had gathered together was shaken, and they were all filled with the Holy Spirit and began to speak the word of God with boldness."
—Acts 4:31 (NASB)

Have you ever noticed that people's expression of the anointing can be messy? Why is that? The wisdom of Solomon in Proverbs 14:4 tells us, *"Where no oxen are, the trough is clean; but much increase comes by the strength of an ox."* Because God has entrusted imperfect people with His anointing, it's never going to be flawless. But that doesn't mean we shouldn't steward the anointed power and presence of God with great care and stay strong amid temptation and tribulation. In this chapter, we'll look at how to yield to the Holy Spirit and cooperate with His anointing, remaining faithful to represent the character of Jesus. What a blessing to be able to walk in the likeness of Christ!

CALLING AND PRAYING FOR THE SPIRIT'S PRESENCE

Perhaps you have been in a church meeting where the minister has said, "Come, Holy Spirit." When someone publicly makes this invitation, that person is calling for the Spirit's *manifest* presence. Although God is present everywhere all the time (He is omnipresent), the intensity of His presence is not always apparent tangibly. If we are to cooperate with the anointing of the Spirit, we must first welcome the Holy Spirit in a more tangible way.

When this happens, a variety of things can occur. Those present might start to sense or feel the Spirit come upon them, or they might not feel a thing. Others may feel like a bucket of fire has been dumped on them. They might even scream, which can alarm the person standing near them who is trying to figure out if what is happening is from God or the devil, or if the person is just performing a show! In the same moment, a few others may have gone into prayer because they're engaging as intercessory watchmen over what's going on. Then there might be others who are just observing because this is all brand-new to them. And let's not forget those who may be so hungry for God that they're just lost in worship. They have tears streaming down their face and are not paying attention to anyone else.

All this might be going on just because someone with a dimension of spiritual authority has said something like, "Come, Holy Spirit." With this invitation and call, these diverse, natural and supernatural, physical and soulish, and maybe even demonic, activities have been stirred up. Wow! What is happening?

Many people have concerns over this phenomenon of asking the Holy Spirit to come and seeing such results. Some wonder if, in this way, we're "commanding" God or if we even need to invite the Spirit to come. But God desires to manifest Himself among us as we seek Him, and we can reach out to Him as we learn to discern the true manifestations from the false or demonic.

I believe that calling for the Holy Spirit's presence may include the following:

- An intercessory plea
- A "welcome mat" being put out
- A declaration of faith that the person calling for God's presence is walking in, which possibly others are not
- An acknowledgement of what is already occurring supernaturally
- A proclamation of what is not yet, but what is to come

While we can call for the Holy Spirit to come, we can also pray for the Holy Spirit to be "released." Although, at times, the Spirit "fell" sovereignly and spontaneously (see Acts 2:2; 10:44), there were other times when the disciples prayed for the Holy Spirit to be poured out. Today, we, also, may proceed to do this with confidence, for seven main reasons:

1. The Scriptures teach us that we can ask for the Holy Spirit. (See, for example, Luke 11:13.)
2. The church needs power and was first empowered when the Holy Spirit came upon the followers of Jesus. (See Acts 1:8; 2:4.)
3. The growth of the early church was triggered by a manifestation of God's power through signs and wonders. (See Acts 5:12–16.)
4. Paul, despite his gift for brilliant reasoning, rated demonstrations of God's power more highly than just the preaching of the gospel. (See 1 Corinthians 2:4.)
5. Miracles, signs, and wonders were released by the power of God to confirm the preaching of the gospel. (See, for example, Mark 16:20; Acts 14:3; Hebrews 2:3–4.)

6. The anointing of power through the Holy Spirit accomplishes the release of the gifts of the Spirit and allows God to initiate spiritual ministry. (See 1 Corinthians 12:7–11.)[5]

7. Experientially, the Holy Spirit releases blessing, anointing, and ministry. The gospel is confirmed, the kingdom of God is extended, and Jesus is magnified.

No matter what is happening—something peaceful or something wild—if Jesus is not in the middle of it, you don't want to be a part of it. But if Jesus is in the middle of it, don't you want to be a part of whatever the Holy Spirit is doing?

YIELDING THE NATURAL MIND TO THE SUPERNATURAL WAYS OF GOD

Proverbs 3:5 instructs us, *"Trust in the L*ORD *with all your heart, and lean not on your own understanding."* Why aren't we supposed to *lean* on our own understanding? Because it can be unstable and may move! The natural mind can also get into a tug-of-war with the heart. This is not to demean the mind, particularly the renewed mind in Christ. But what must win out is the heart of God in union with the heart of a man or a woman of God. This is what helps us to stand strong in the anointing.

At times, I have challenged some very brilliant people that the voice of their heart needs to speak louder than the voice of their mind. Here are four pieces of wisdom to help you choose to cooperate with the anointing and the supernatural ways of God:

1. Understand that welcoming the Holy Spirit with no agenda of our own is an uncomfortable ministry style. You're just going to have to get used to it.

---

5. For more on this topic, please see my book *Releasing Spiritual Gifts Today* (New Kensington, PA: Whitaker House, 2016).

2. Accept that God can be very unpredictable. Think of the many supernatural occurrences throughout the Bible. Are they what you would have expected?

3. Realize that God's workings can often be untidy. That's why 1 Corinthians 14:40 tells us, *"Let all things be done decently and in order."* Let's slow down and make sure we see what this verse says: *"Let all things be done…."* All things. God's idea of order, however, is not necessarily man's idea of order.

4. Let God be God. If we want God to fit into our box and give us what we want the way we want it, then we're looking for a god that is more like Santa Claus.

HUMAN RESPONSES TO GOD'S POWER

If we are going to cooperate with the anointing and not quench the Spirit, we need to know how people may respond. A response to the anointing that gets a lot of attention is falling in the Spirit. Different terms have been used throughout church history for this phenomenon. Much of this terminology is human phraseology and even slang to try to describe the indescribable. Sometimes people add their own ingredients to what the Holy Spirit is doing, yet we don't need to help the Holy Spirit at all. Here is a list of some of the phrases that people from different backgrounds and denominations have used:

- Falling
- Being slain
- Slayed/slain in the Spirit
- Resting in the Spirit (I relate to this phrase the most.)
- Swooning (This term appears in revival and awakening journals.)
- Zapped

- Overcome by the Spirit (People in past revivals used this expression a lot.)

- Overpowered

- Rapt in ecstasy (This expression was used by Teresa of Ávila, the Carmelite nun.)

- Struck down

- Fainting

- The glory fall (John Wesley used this expression.)

- Having a glory fit (This is some good ol' Pentecostal language.)

- Prostration (This term comes from the book of Daniel.)

- Deep sleep

- Falling under the power

Should we be surprised that the human body responds when it encounters the living God—the One who used only words to create hundreds of billions of galaxies in the universe? We jump when we receive a little shock from static electricity, so getting touched by God will be altogether dynamic. Let's look at a few biblical examples.

In the Old Testament, 2 Chronicles 5:14 explains that *"the priests could not continue ministering because of the cloud; for the glory of the LORD filled the house of God."* The prophets sometimes fell as the Spirit came on them, giving them a vision, a burden, or a message from God. Ezekiel 1:28 (NLT) says, *"This is what the glory of the LORD looked like to me. When I saw it, I fell face down on the ground, and I heard someone's voice speaking to me."* This verse doesn't say that Ezekiel did a courtesy fall into the arms of a catcher. He fell facedown and heard God's voice speaking to him. Daniel had a similar experience. Daniel 10:9 (ESV) says, *"As I heard* the sound of his words, I fell on my face in deep sleep with my face to the ground."

In the New Testament, Matthew 17:6 tells us that the disciples who accompanied Christ *"fell on their faces"* before the transfigured Lord. When people were delivered from demons, it seems they often fell under God's power. (See, for example, Mark 3:11.) John 18 records the time when a crowd of soldiers and officers came looking for Jesus to arrest Him. What happened? *"When He said to them, 'I am He,' they drew back and fell to the ground"* (verse 6).

What about Saul? He and his companions fell to the ground when they saw the light from heaven on the road to Damascus. (See Acts 9:4; 26:14.) This was the response of unbelievers encountering the glory of the Lord. How I long for those who have yet to meet Jesus to encounter Him in this way! Lastly, John wrote what happened when he was taken up in the Spirit and encountered the resurrected Christ: *"When I saw him, I fell at his feet as though dead"* (Revelation 1:17 ESV).

In church history, there are many amazing examples of the manifestations of the Spirit as men and women of God have cooperated with the Holy Spirit. And I'm specifically talking about this "Come, Holy Spirit" realm—fainting, falling, or being overwhelmed. Let's look at a few of these supernatural experiences. I recommend the book *Overcome by the Spirit* by Father Francis MacNutt of the Catholic charismatic movement, which mentions various supernatural manifestations people have experienced, including the following by Teresa of Ávila and Charles Wesley.[6]

Teresa of Ávila was a sixteenth-century Spanish nun, and she wrote this in her autobiography:

> While seeking God in this way, the soul becomes conscious that it is fainting almost completely away, in a kind of swoon, with an

---
6. Francis MacNutt, *Overcome by the Spirit* (Guildford, Surrey, UK: Eagle, 1991).

exceeding great and sweet delight. It gradually ceases to breathe, and all its bodily strength begins to fail it.... It is futile for him to attempt to speak: his mind cannot form a single word, nor, if it could, would he have the strength to pronounce it. For in this condition all outward strength vanishes, while the strength of the soul increases so that it may the better have the fruition of its bliss....

This prayer, for however long it may last, does no harm.... The outward effects are so noteworthy that there can be no doubt some great thing has taken place: we experience a loss of strength but the experience is one of such delight that afterwards our strength grows greater.[7]

Note the various responses that she mentions: swooning, great delight and bliss, loss of speech, loss of body strength, and increased strength in both the soul and the body. Long before Christian charismatic conferences, people earnestly seeking the presence of God encountered Him supernaturally.

Next, read this testimony taken from John Wesley's journal, which shows us the result of the power of God that came upon those united in prayer:

Monday, January 1, 1739. Messrs. Hall, Kinchin, Ingham, Whitefield, Hutchins, and my brother Charles, were present at our love-feast in Fetterlans, with about sixty of our brethren. At three in the morning, as we were continuing instant in prayer, the power of God come mightily upon us, insomuch that many cried out for exceeding joy, and many fell to the ground. As soon as we were recovered a little from that awe and amazement at

---

7. *The Life of Teresa of Jesus*, translated by E. Allison Peers (Garden City, NY: Image Books, 1960), 177–178.

the presence of his Majesty, we broke out with one voice, *We praise thee, O God: we acknowledge thee to be the Lord.*[8]

As I described in my book *Revival Breakthrough*, Charles G. Finney was instrumental in the Second Great Awakening, an American revival in the mid-1800s. He was a lawyer before he became a noted evangelist, and he was referred to as a "logician on fire." That designation indicates the blending of his natural gifts with the fire of the Holy Spirit. Here is what he wrote about the impact of his supernatural encounter with Jesus:

> As I went in and shut the door after me, it seemed as if I met the Lord Jesus Christ face to face. It did not occur to me then, nor did it for some time afterward, that it was wholly a mental state. On the contrary, it seemed to me that I met Him face to face and saw Him as I would see any other man. He said nothing, but looked at me in such a manner as to break me right down at His feet. I have always since regarded this as a most remarkable state of mind, for it seemed to me a reality that He stood before me and that I fell down at His feet and poured out my soul to Him. I wept aloud like a child, and made such confessions as I could with my choked utterance. It seemed to me as if I bathed His feet with my tears....
>
> ...The Holy Spirit descended upon me in a manner that seemed to go through me, body and soul. I could feel the impression, like a wave of electricity, going through and through me. Indeed it seemed to come in waves, and waves of liquid love—for I could not express it in any other way. And yet it did not seem like water, but rather as the breath of God. I can recollect

---

8. "An Extract of the Rev. Mr. John Wesley's Journals, Volume I," in the digital collection Evans Early American Imprint Collection, University of Michigan Library Digital Collections, 224–225, https://quod.lib.umich.edu/cgi/t/text/text-idx?c=evans;cc=evans;idno=N22587.0001.001;q1=love-feast;rgn=div1;type=simple;view=text;subview=detail;node=N22587.0001.001:18. Italics are in the original.

distinctly that it seemed to fan me like immense wings; and it seemed to me, as these waves passed over me, that they literally moved my hair like a passing breeze.

No words can express the wonderful love that was shed abroad in my heart. It seemed to me that I should burst. I wept aloud with joy and love, and I do not know but I should say I literally bellowed out the unutterable gushings of my heart. These waves came over me, and over me, and over me one after the other, until I recollect I cried out, "I shall die if these waves continue to pass over me." I said to the Lord, "Lord, I cannot bear any more." Yet I had no fear of death....[9]

RESPONDING TO MOVES OF GOD

Because I can be very logically oriented, sometimes it can take a while to persuade me of something, including the spiritual reality of certain manifestations. In the winter of 1993, the Holy Spirit specifically addressed me. He needed to. I was observing manifestations occurring in different pockets of a move of the Holy Spirit through various people's ministries. I'd already been around the operation of the different gifts of the Holy Spirit, but I was now seeing new fire-starters—people showing up on the scene with different ways of operating.

For a while, I was uncertain about these manifestations. I wasn't ready to fully engage in everything that I saw, but that's not wrong. You could call that discernment. Then the Holy Spirit said to me, "If you can't jump in the middle of it, bless it. And if you can't bless it, gently observe it. But if you can't simply observe it, then just don't criticize what you don't understand."

This is an admonition for us to observe concerning the anointed power and the manifest presence of the Holy Spirit. This word of

---

9. Charles Finney, *The Memoirs of Charles G. Finney*, 1868, https://www.charlesgfinney.com/memoirsrestored/memrest02.htm.

wisdom helped me significantly, and I hope it helps you too. Once again, I encourage you to jump into whatever you see the Holy Spirit doing. But if you're struggling to bless what you do not understand, gently observe. If you can't do that, avoid criticism.

What is the lesson to learn here? When a person encounters the living God, watch out! You can expect God to do something. But also know that people will not always respond to the anointing in ways as demonstrative as I've shared. Fruit of the Spirit like love, peace, patience, and joy can also be present, and these are no less divine encounters with God.

MINISTERING THE ANOINTING THROUGH PRAYER

In over fifty years of vocational ministry, I have ministered and watched others minister the anointing in very diverse ways as we've sought to cooperate with what we perceive the Holy Spirit wants to do. Here are some ways to pray as you follow the Holy Spirit:

Pray by what you see in the natural that the Holy Spirit is doing. I've just shared some very demonstrative ways people can react to the anointing of the Spirit after someone has called forth the Spirit to be released. Your role is then to bless what you observe the Father doing. That can be as simple as saying, "I bless what You are doing. More, Lord." You can then continue to observe and bless the natural effects upon people as the Holy Spirit moves.

Pray by what you see with your spiritual eyes. The Holy Spirit desires to show you what He wants to do. In this type of prayer, you may see pictures or visions, receive an impression or an unction, or perceive with your spiritual or natural senses. You then invoke the Lord's presence on what you discern He wants to do. This is praying by spiritual insight or revelatory prayer.

Pray by faith. We can pray for people because the Bible tells us to do it! James 5:14–15 instructs us in what to do if someone is sick: call for the elders of the church to pray for them and anoint them with oil. *"And the prayer of faith will save the sick, and the Lord will raise him up"* (verse 15). This passage doesn't say you need to schedule a healing crusade, recruit intercessors to bathe the event in prayer, and have an anointed worship team to create the right environment for healing. I believe in these helpful activities and have participated in them. But what I want to emphasize here is that although you may not feel or sense anything, or you're just on your own with a colleague or someone you've just met, you can act in raw obedience to the Scriptures. Here we must take a risk and step out in faith. We listen and then obey. This is how we can show our love for Jesus. (See John 14:21, 23.)

INCREASING IN THE ANOINTING

As we learn to cooperate with the Holy Spirit and minister the anointing, God will challenge us to increase in the anointing. Here are four keys for increasing in the anointing.

1. FAITHFULNESS

Jesus taught His disciples that faithfulness brings increase. Look with me at Luke 16:10–12 (NIV):

> *Whoever can be trusted with very little can also be trusted with much, and whoever is dishonest with very little will also be dishonest with much. So if you have not been trustworthy in handling worldly wealth, who will trust you with true riches? And if you have not been trustworthy with someone else's property, who will give you property of your own?*

A saying I have owned for myself is, "If you are faithful with little, you will be given much. If you are faithful in that which is another's, you will be given your own. And if you are faithful in the natural, you will become a ruler over true spiritual riches." As a person who was born in Cowgill, Missouri, population 259, I didn't start with much. I've often said that I'm a nobody from nowhere. But I am also an example of a person who was given a little bit and was faithful with it. I want you to know that faithfulness is a key for increase in any area of life, not just the anointing or the supernatural. Faithfulness matters.

2. ASSOCIATION

Those with whom you walk will impact you. You will increase in the anointing by hanging out with those who love the anointing and walk faithfully with the Holy Spirit. Ask the Lord for mentors—those whom you can get to know personally. But you may never meet in person some mentors the Lord will put in your life through their resources, such as books, podcasts, videos, and other teachings. Watch, observe, and learn from those who know the ways of the Lord. It really makes a difference.

3. ENVIRONMENT

An area, region, or congregation can have an atmosphere of faith and expectancy in God or of unbelief and indifference to the Spirit. You will increase in the anointing by being in the right environment or atmosphere where faith, hope, and love are valued. This is why being part of a vibrant local gathering of believers is so important. While it is good to be influenced by other parts of the body of Christ (today, the ease of travel and the instant connection of the Internet give us almost unlimited access to fellowships of believers around the world), a local expression is essential to remain anchored in the Word and the Spirit.

4. INFLUENCE

What are the main things you spend your time doing? What you give your time and attention to most will greatly influence your desires and inner motivations. Electronic smart devices monopolize so much of our time these days—usually in the form of our scrolling through random content that entertains but does not feed our spirits. Be a student of revival history. Study and meditate on the Word of God. Let's invite Jesus to be our greatest influence through fellowship with Him, other godly connections, and faith-filled activities. What goes in will come out, so watch your influences if you want to increase in the anointing.

PRACTICAL POINTS FOR PROTECTING THE ANOINTING

Cooperating with the anointing of the Holy Spirit doesn't have to be complicated. God wants to move in people's lives even more than we want Him to. He's not looking for you to get to some elevated spiritual level before He can use you to minister to others. Sometimes we can forget the simple things that help us to walk faithfully in the anointing. Let me share seven practical tips.

1. Acknowledge the call of God on your own life. See what God has given to you and put it to work in faith. *"We are God's handiwork, created in Christ Jesus to do good works"* (Ephesians 2:10 NIV).

2. Get rest so you can be filled back up. Having a weekly day of rest was a part of God's Ten Commandments for a reason.

3. Pull away for a while. Sometimes we need extended times of rest and rejuvenation. This is both godly and biblical. God has the world firmly in His grasp, and it will not fall apart if you pull away to prioritize time with family or friends for your personal well-being.

4. Get an outlet or hobby outside of what could be called "ministry." Learn to laugh. Remember, the fruit of the Spirit includes joy, and *"a joyful heart is good medicine"* (Proverbs 17:22, various translations).

5. Don't take yourself too seriously. The mistakes we make—big and small—are a part of the process of learning to cooperate with the Holy Spirit. Continue to step out in faith even when things don't happen the way you expected. It's not about you anyway!

6. Be a person of persistence and perseverance. Don't give up! Remember the admonition and promise of Galatians 6:9: *"Let us not grow weary while doing good, for in due season we shall reap if we do not lose heart."*

7. Focus on Jesus and be Christlike! This is probably the best way to stand strong in the anointing. Jesus is our ultimate reward. We aren't primarily endeavoring to be anointed or release supernatural encounters. Our reward is Jesus, and only Jesus.

GOING FOR "THE DOUBLE"

Cooperating with the anointing to experience divine encounters is more than seeing supernatural things happen in your life or receiving answers to your prayers. I've met many anointed people who have walked in supernatural power and performed extraordinary miracles. But only some have pursued what I call "the double."

Years ago, on Mother's Day, I prayed a special prayer for my wife. During the prayer, I saw in a vision a picture of the clear crystal pitcher I had purchased for her in the Czech Republic years before. Etched on the pitcher was the number nine to the second power: 9^2. This pitcher tipped, and water began to pour into her. I understood that the water was the water of God's Word, and the work of the Spirit that would come out of her was as crystal clear as what was going into her. But I was puzzled by the 9^2. I asked the Lord, "What is this?" I felt the Holy Spirit speak to me, "We're going for the double."

What is "the double"? He said, "We're going for character to carry the power." So what does 9^2 mean? The nine represents the nine gifts of the Holy Spirit from 1 Corinthians 12, the fullness of the power of God.[10] God wants us to ask, seek, and knock on His door for "more, Lord!" (See, for example, Matthew 7:7.) But we're also going for fullness of character. That's why the nine is squared. The nine aspects of the fruit of the Holy Spirit represent the character of Christ that we desire to bear so we can carry the nine gifts of the Spirit.

Did you know that the various fruit of the Holy Spirit are just as supernatural as the gifts of the Holy Spirit? I have become so convinced of this that I dedicated an entire chapter to this theme in my pioneer book *The Feeler*.[11] I teach that our goal must be to have gifts that bear good fruit. In fact, I think the double refers to having new wineskins for the new wine. Yes, our goal is to develop the character of Christ *and* to earnestly desire the fullness of the power of God in operation for the glory of God. Cooperating with the Holy Spirit to release the anointing for divine encounters must mean that we are going for the double: character that can carry the gifts—gifts that bear long-term fruit. When we seek and demonstrate the double, we are able to stand strong in the anointing.

PRAYER TO FLOW WITH THE ANOINTING

Heavenly Father, I want to learn to flow in the supernatural anointing of the Holy Spirit. I put out a welcome mat for the Spirit right now. Come, Holy Spirit. I need more of Your gifts, presence, and power. Move in, upon, and through me with greater effectiveness and impact. I hunger to do the *"greater works"* mentioned in John 14:12 so that Jesus Christ can receive the reward of His suffering. I long to be among a generation that cooperates with Your Word, will, and ways. I want "the

---

10. For more on this subject, see my book and study guide entitled *Releasing Spiritual Gifts Today*.
11. James Goll, *The Feeler* (New Kensington, PA: Whitaker House, 2021).

double" in both the fruit and the gifts of the Spirit. I am hungry for more of Your touch upon my life. Send more of Your anointing upon me. Amen and amen!

4

DECEIVED WHILE YET ANOINTED?

"And she said, 'The Philistines are upon you, Samson!'
So he awoke from his sleep, and said, 'I will go out as before,
at other times, and shake myself free!'
But he did not know that the LORD had departed from him."
—Judges 16:20

I have been waiting for years to unpack this teaching on deception related to the anointing. *Hold on. Wait a minute! What? Mr. James W. Goll, someone who has stood for strong and sound doctrine, are you saying, "There's deception in the precious and pure anointing of the Holy Spirit"?* Well, another way to say it is that deception can come from our misconceptions when touching and handling the anointing. The anointing itself is not deceptive in the least bit, but you can be both anointed and deceived at the same time. The long list of influential leaders and ministers who operated powerfully in the anointing while living in known, egregious sin shows this to be true. In order to stand strong in the anointing, we must be able to discern the traps that can come from the enemy while we are walking in the midst of supernatural encounters.

This teaching may save your life. For sure, it will help unravel confusion about why people who are highly gifted think they can get away with immorality, and why highly gifted people can have wrong doctrines and still see godly fruit produced by their ministries. The anointing is not God's seal of approval on a person's character or doctrine. The anointing is a gift, and a gift is purely by grace, which means that no one earns it or deserves it. We do a great disservice to gifted people by elevating them to pedestals that we should never put them on.

With these hints of where we're going, you can see why I have been so burdened about this subject—having studied it in Scripture, looked at it from precedents in Jewish and church history, and been involved in moves of the Holy Spirit for decades. There is so much debris today from casualties of despair, disappointment, and disillusionment that have been caused by fallen, anointed vessels of God. The good news is that the Bible is not afraid to address this subject. The Word of God openly deals with a lot of things that we are often afraid to address.

LESSONS FROM THE LIFE OF SAMSON

When you think of Samson, the famous muscle-bound judge in the Old Testament, what words would you use to describe his calling? Two positive words that may come to mind for this great deliverer of Israel are *strength* and *justice*. Usually, another person's name also comes to mind when we think of Samson: Delilah. Although Samson's original calling was to purity, he is a classic example of how someone can be deceived while yet anointed and what we must to do (and not do) to stand strong. Samson tragically fell into a trap of being deceived and misled while under the anointing, resulting in a spiral of chaos that only God could redeem. Let's look at his story and some lessons we can learn from it.

Judges 13 describes how Samson's birth came about. The Bible says that his parents had no children because his mother was barren. The angel of the Lord appeared to Samson's mother and said,

> *You are barren and childless, but you are going to become pregnant and give birth to a son. Now see to it that you drink no wine or other fermented drink and that you do not eat anything unclean. You will become pregnant and have a son whose head is never to be touched by a razor because the boy is to be a Nazirite, dedicated to God from the womb. He will take the lead in delivering Israel from the hands of the Philistines.* (Judges 13:3–5 NIV)

Note the supernatural activity surrounding Samson's birth! His parents experienced an angelic visitation and healing from infertility. We can also see Samson's consecration and calling. He was a Nazirite from the womb—holy, set apart unto God, as proclaimed by the angel of the Lord. Fascinating. What else does the Bible have to say about Samson? *"So the woman bore a son and called his name Samson; and the child grew, and the Lord blessed him. And the Spirit of the Lord began to move upon him"* (verses 24–25). The beginning of Samson's life sounds a lot like that of Samuel, John the Baptist, and even Jesus. Sadly, not everyone who starts well finishes well.

Judges 14–16 records the rest of Samson's story, which is an enlightening account of his triumphant rise, devastating fall, and redemptive end as a leader of Israel. As we go through parts of his story, I will highlight key lessons so we can discern the traps the enemy lays out for us and learn how we can stand strong in the anointing.

THE ENEMY SEARCHES FOR THE KEY

I believe that every person is anointed for a specific purpose. God has called you for something special, and there is a distinct key to your anointing. If you don't know what that key is, you may need to search it out. I think one of my keys has been the consistent practice of praying in tongues. Many years ago, the Lord told me that if I would pray in the gift of tongues for two hours at a time, He would give me revelation. Now, I don't tell other people, "If you'll do this, you'll get what I got." This is a distinct key for me that is tied to my personal relationship with the Lord.

However, we all have similar general keys available to us—like faithfulness as we walk in the fruit of the Spirit, the confirmation of the Word, and perhaps angelic activity. But what is the key that is unique to you? Samson had his: it was his hair. He had a hairy anointing! Samson's hair remaining uncut was the special, mysterious key that was part of his Nazarite vow. But Samson also had an Achilles' heel (to borrow a concept from Greek mythology). The realm of the flesh—specifically an attraction to foreign, beautiful women who did not follow the Lord— was Samson's place of vulnerability. As the enemy searched for how he could undermine the anointing of this up-and-coming judge, he found it. Everyone has a personal key *and* a place of vulnerability.

Reviewing Samson's life, we quickly see that he loved the world and the things of the world. (Contrast 1 John 2:15.) Judges 14–15 describes Samson's first love interest: a young Philistine woman. Samson demanded that his parents go and get her for him as his wife despite their direct counsel against it. (See Judges 14:2–3.) Growing up as an Israelite, Samson would have been very aware of the evil practices of the Philistines and of the law of Moses that prohibited marrying foreign women. (See Deuteronomy 7:1, 3–4.) While God used this relationship to bring justice against the Philistines, we see the enemy's initial attempts to wear Samson down and lure him through his lustful affections.

During a feast before his wedding, Samson posed a riddle with a wager to thirty companions who had gathered to celebrate, betting thirty linen garments and thirty changes of clothing that they could not guess the answer within a week. The riddle was based on a recent lion attack Samson had averted as the Spirit of the Lord came upon him mightily. He had ripped apart the young lion with his bare hands! Who does that? Unable to solve the riddle, the companions badgered Samson's wife to press him for the answer, *"or else we will burn you and your father's house with fire"* (Judges 14:15). The Bible says that *"she had wept on him the seven days while their feast lasted"* (verse 17), saying, *"You only hate me! You do not love me!"* (verse 16). Finally, *"it happened on the seventh day that he told her, because she pressed him so much"* (verse 17). Can you feel how the enemy is searching for the best way to wear Samson down?

Samson's wife told the men the answer to the riddle, and so Samson lost the bet. To make good on his promise, Samson went down to a nearby town of the Philistines and *"killed thirty of their men, took their apparel, and gave the changes of clothing to those who had explained the riddle"* (verse 19). Even as Samson pursued the desires of his flesh, the Spirit of the Lord came mightily upon him with superhuman strength to execute justice. Because of Samson's anger over the event, he went back to his parents' home. The Bible says that the father of Samson's wife then gave her to Samson's best man.

You can imagine what happened when Samson returned to the woman a while later and discovered she was no longer his wife. To say that Samson was upset would be a gross understatement. Samson had no ordinary mood swing! His hand-to-hand combat gets a lot of attention. But how about his ability to catch three hundred foxes and tie them tail to tail in pairs? After Samson found out that his Philistine wife had been given to another man, *"he took torches, turned the foxes tail to tail, and put a torch between each pair of tails. When he had set the torches on fire, he let the foxes go into the standing grain of the Philistines"* (Judges 15:4–5). When the Philistines retaliated by burning the woman and her father with fire, Samson *"attacked the Philistines with great fury and killed many of them"* (verse 8 NLT). Samson was on a roll, wreaking havoc against the Philistines! But he was also compromising his Nazarite call, and the devil was observing how he could bind Samson.

The Philistines went to make war against Judah, and the men of Judah asked them why they were so intent on attacking them. The answer: Samson! So, three thousand men from Judah went to find Samson to arrest him. Samson asked not to be killed by his Israelite brothers, and they replied, *"'No, but we will tie you securely and deliver you into [the Philistines'] hand; but we will surely not kill you.' And they bound him with two new ropes and brought him up from the rock"* (verse 13).

When the Philistines saw him, they *"came shouting against him. Then the Spirit of the LORD came mightily upon him; and the ropes that were on his arms became like flax that is burned with fire, and his bonds broke loose from his hands. He found a fresh jawbone of a donkey, reached out his hand and took it, and killed a thousand men with it"* (Judges 15:14–15). The devil certainly learned that two ropes were not going to bind Samson. He also saw that Samson wanted two worlds: the realm of the Spirit and the realm of the flesh. Samson was fulfilling God's desire to confront the Philistines (see Judges 14:4), but he was also falling into a deception of the anointing: thinking he could get away with sin. At least that's what Samson thought for a season.

A key truth to remember is that we don't normally reap in the present season what we sow in this season, so we think we can get away with sin. You could be walking in a powerful anointing, seeing signs and wonders, and still be in sin. You may think, "I can walk in adultery, be watching porn, or get drunk and even prophesy with looseness." While you don't reap in this season what you're sowing in this season, you will reap it in another season. What you're reaping in this season could be because of what you sowed in a previous season—your fasting, prayer, and seeking of God. And now you're reaping the fruit of that season, enjoying the glory of God.

So, Samson began to play with the anointing. He was thinking, "There may be a thousand Philistines, but they can't touch me. I'll just grab this jawbone of a dead donkey and take them out." What confidence Samson had in the power of the anointing, to think he could single-handedly take out one thousand warriors with an improvised weapon!

You, too, are called and gifted and anointed. Because *"the gifts and the calling of God are irrevocable"* (Romans 11:29), you may see a crowd of people, receive words of knowledge, and call out specific details about certain individuals' lives that only God could have known. Why does God give the keys to His "sports car" to teenagers whose brains aren't fully developed? We think it shouldn't work that way. People should have to go through trials and pass tests and develop humility first! But God calls us and gives us gifts. We don't earn anything. We only receive God's grace—but our character does matter to Him.

If we are honest with ourselves, most of us want both worlds. That's why we have to die to self every day. There is a part of every one of us that wants some glory, some credit. Your pocket of temptation won't necessarily be the same as someone else's because your Achilles' heel might not be the same as someone else's. But hallelujah! We also have a higher divine nature that is stronger than the flesh. Galatians 2:20 (NLT) declares, *"My old self has been crucified with Christ. It is no longer I who live, but Christ lives in me. So I live in this earthly body by trusting in the Son of God, who loved me and gave himself for me."*

Ecclesiastes 8:11–13 declares another truth to remember:

Because the sentence against an evil work is not executed speedily, therefore the heart of the sons of men is fully set in them to do evil. Though a sinner does evil a hundred times, and his days are prolonged, yet I surely know that it will be well with those who fear God, who fear before Him. But it will not be well with the wicked; nor will he prolong his days, which are as a shadow, because he does not fear before God.

We can deceive ourselves over the delay of God's judgment on our sin. We may think that the presence of the anointing is God's endorsement of our character. The truth is that the presence of the anointing is a sign of God's mercy on us and of grace toward those He wants us to bless.

Samson's demonstrative success led him astray; he thought he could do whatever he wanted. Judges 16:1–3 (GNT) continues to unravel Samson's deception:

One day Samson went to the Philistine city of Gaza, where he met a prostitute and went to bed with her. The people of Gaza found out that Samson was there, so they surrounded the place and waited for him all night long at the city gate. They were quiet all night, thinking to themselves, "We'll wait until daybreak, and then we'll kill him." But Samson stayed in bed only until midnight. Then he got up and took hold of the city gate and pulled it up—doors, posts, lock, and all. He put them on his shoulders and carried them far off to the top of the hill overlooking Hebron.

Watch this. Samson sleeps with a prostitute. Hello! The Bible has some X-rated places! When Samson is done with his night of pleasure, he discovers he's stuck inside the city. What does he do? With supernatural strength, he pulls up the city gates—the Bible emphasizes "*doors, posts, lock, and all.*" With that feat of superhuman strength, Samson heads toward his ultimate fall in the hands of Delilah, woman number three. (See verse 4.) At least that's the number the Bible records. There might have been more.

Is it clear yet that the enemy lures those whom he sees are anointed? When the Philistine lords learned that Samson was in love with Delilah, they said to her, *"Entice him, and see where his great strength lies and how we can overpower him so that we may bind him to humble him"* (Judges 16:5 NASB). Did you catch that? The goal was to entice Samson, overpower him, bind him, and humble him. The enemy is trying to find Samson's arrogant weakness and wedge his way in.

The devil's plot goes beyond getting you to have a one-night fling or to struggle with some repetitive sin that brings some guilt and shame. He wants to find out the key to your anointing and destroy you. Each of the leaders offered to pay Delilah eleven hundred pieces of silver. If there were only three Philistine leaders who came to Delilah (there were most likely more), in today's value, that would be about $40,000. The enemy is willing to pay big to take you out!

Can you see the spiritual warfare involved? There was a conspiracy, a demonic plot against Samson. And there is one against you! Experiencing spiritual warfare, however, isn't an excuse not to take personal responsibility for your choices. Yet when you start to play with the anointing, deception sets in. Then the enemy leans on another devious tactic: the persistent wearing down of a saint.

THE ENEMY'S PERSISTENCE IN WEARING DOWN

In Judges 16:6–7 (NIV), we see the beginning of the drawn-out process in which Samson is worn down: *"So Delilah said to Samson, 'Tell me the secret of your great strength and how you can be tied up and subdued.' Samson answered her, 'If anyone ties me with seven fresh bowstrings that have not been dried, I'll become as weak as any other man.'"* He's remembering the two new ropes he snapped like charred flax, the city gates he lifted over his head like a boy's barbell, and the men he killed without breaking a sweat. How easy it would be to think, "I am indestructible." This is confirmed when the lords of the Philistines give Delilah seven fresh bowstrings, and she binds Samson and then warns him that the Philistines are in the room. As before, Samson breaks the bowstrings "*as a strand of yarn breaks when it touches fire. So the secret of his strength was not known*" (verse 9).

The persistent wearing down continues, and Samson continues to play on the edge of the cliff. The Bible doesn't say that he was napping when Delilah bound him the first time. Perhaps they were just playing around. Samson was just having some fun with Delilah, taking a break from being the judge of Israel, but the Bible says that "*men were lying in wait, staying with her in the room*" (verse 9). Are you getting the picture of how the enemy works?

Samson is sliding down an evil slope, moving closer to his demise. We can think we are getting away with sin, and we can become proud, but the question is not whether we'll get caught today but where we will be five years from now. The book of Judges says twice that Samson judged Israel for twenty years. *Twenty* years! You can see why it would be easy to be deceived when "*the sentence against an evil work is not executed speedily,*" as we read earlier from Ecclesiastes 8:11.

So Samson breaks the bowstrings, and the secret of his strength is not yet known. But his enemies are getting closer…and closer. Then Delilah says to Samson, "*Look, you have mocked me and told me lies. Now, please tell me what you may be bound with*" (Judges 16:10). Persistence, persistence, persistence. More accusations and emotions with which to wear down Samson.

Since the new-rope scheme had worked for Samson earlier, he assured Delilah that if he were bound with ropes that had never been used, he would be like any other man. These Philistines must not have heard that Samson had easily snapped two new ropes before he slaughtered the one thousand Philistines.

Delilah binds Samson with new ropes and warns Samson about the Philistines, who are in the room waiting. Either they are really quiet or Samson is not paying attention! Wake up, Samson! Not to fear; Samson breaks the ropes like a thread. But Delilah gets closer to knowing the truth of his strength. She presses him again, and, this time, Samson crosses a line. He allows Delilah to toy around with the source of his anointing—his hair—saying, *"If you weave the seven locks of my head into the web of the loom…"* (verse 13). The enemy is getting closer. Why? Daniel 7:25 speaks of a future time when the enemy will wear down the saints and prevail for a time. Wear down. Wear down. We must be aware of the wearing down of the saints.

When Delilah wakes Samson to warn him about the Philistines, Samson dismantles the trap and moves on with his day. Delilah has had enough and unloads on Samson. Carefully read the following from Judges 16:15–17:

> *Then she said to him, "How can you say, 'I love you,' when your heart is not with me? You have mocked me these three times, and have not told me where your great strength lies." And it came to pass, when she pestered him daily with her words and pressed him, so that his soul was vexed to death, that he told her all his heart, and said to her, "No razor has ever come upon my head, for I have been a Nazirite to God from my mother's womb. If I am shaven, then my strength will leave me, and I shall become weak, and be like any other man."*

The enemy can be very subtle. He talks to you in a way that you eventually buy into: "You're all alone. You used to be on the A-list for ministry, but no one thinks of you much anymore. People have forgotten you. There's not much to look forward to." I hear these thoughts like the rest of you, and, with these little kernels of truth, the enemy tempts us to believe they are the whole truth. But that's how the devil communicates. The evil one speaks enough truth, or we would never listen. Right? He catches our attention, and then this trickster of an enemy slips in a little lie mingled with the truth, and we have gulped it down before we have had the time to discern what's really going on. This chameleon serpent does his tricks over again and again. It's a pattern of wrapping the truth in a lie.

He also speaks in first person. Did you know that? Yes, he uses the first person and says, "I'm alone. I'm rejected. I'm cut off. People used to want me, but I am no longer wanted. I used to be.... I'll never be...." The sad truth is that we think these messages are about us, but they are not. Satan is talking about himself because he was once a covering cherub over the music of heaven. (See Ezekiel 28:13–14.) He was an A-list angel who lost his place and got booted out. But we hear his words in the first person and assign them to ourselves.

The enemy is persistent—very persistent—to wear us down until we are *"vexed to death"* and finally let go of it all. And that's what Samson did. He eventually became so exhausted that he told Delilah the key to his anointing. She knew that he had shared with her all his heart. They finally had him.

You have to be careful whom you trust with your heart's secrets. Why does Samson let down his guard? Out of weariness. None of us is exempt from this vulnerability. We wrestle with busy schedules, life's complications, physical challenges, emotional and mental instability, and sexual issues. We all can deceive ourselves, hide destructive secrets, and eventually lose any strength to remain in the truth and fight.

Judges 16:19–21 describes possibly the saddest and most frightening fall of any man in Scripture:

> *Then she lulled him to sleep on her knees, and called for a man and had him shave off the seven locks of his head. Then she began to torment him, and his strength left him. And she said, "The Philistines are upon you, Samson!" So he awoke from his sleep, and said, "I*

will go out as before, at other times, and shake myself free!" But he did not know that the LORD *had departed from him. Then the Philistines took him and put out his eyes, and brought him down to Gaza. They bound him with bronze fetters, and he became a grinder in the prison.*

You might say, "God doesn't ever leave us or forsake us." (See, for example, Deuteronomy 31:6.) Although God was still present in Samson's life, Samson's anointing had lifted. It was gone. He lost his covering. He lost his hair, his strength, and his joy. He lost his sight. He lost his purpose. He was left grinding at a mill in a prison. Sadly, this can describe some churches, ministries, businesses, and people. All that remains is a skeleton or a shadow of the authentic creation that God has called them to be. They're living in the smoke of yesterday's fire and cannot discern the traps of the enemy or embrace the blessings of what God wants to do in their lives.

THE MERCY OF GOD AT WORK

There is always hope. Judges 16:22 says, *"However, the hair of his head began to grow again after it had been shaven."* That is a big *however* after such a great fall. His hair began to grow again. When? Right after it had been shaved. This is the mercy of God.

The last verses of Judges 16 reveal the final day of Samson's life. The lords of the Philistines were having a party to offer a sacrifice to their god Dagon and to celebrate Samson's defeat. *"All the lords of the Philistines were there—about three thousand men and women"* (verse 27). They called out, "Bring back that weak, bald man, and let him perform for us!" After his performance, Samson asked a boy to place him between the two main pillars that supported the temple. (See verses 23–27.)

*Then Samson called to the L*ORD*, saying, "O Lord G*OD*, remember me, I pray! Strengthen me, I pray, just this once, O God, that I may with one blow take vengeance on the Philistines for my two eyes!" And Samson took hold of the two middle pillars which supported the temple, and he braced himself against them, one on his right and the other on his left. Then Samson said, "Let me die with the Philistines!" And he pushed with all his might, and the temple fell on the lords and all the people who were in it. So the dead that he killed at his death were more than he had killed in his life.*

(Judges 16:28–30)

What an unnecessary high price to pay, and what a glorious and poor way to end up. Yet Samson's final act of his calling was fulfilled, upheld, and strengthened by the great, great, great grace and mercy of God, the God of redemption. The key to Samson's anointing was restored, his strength returned, his purpose was renewed, and the enemy did not have the final say. May the Lord be glorified even when we fail.

PRAYER FOR FREEDOM FROM DECEPTION

Heavenly Father, I admit that I cannot do anything without You. Forgive me in every area where I have sinned—intentionally and unintentionally—and fallen short of Your glory, and for the ways in which I have fallen into deception because I have sought my own pleasure. Expose every demonic plot set against me, in the mighty name of Jesus Christ! Deliver me from evil and keep me by Your divine grace. I rise up and declare, according to Philippians 4:13, that I can face all things through Christ who strengthens me. I pray for a hedge of protection from deception around my life and that You would enable me to both start and finish well in character and in power, all for Your glory. Amen and amen!

5

PROTECTING THE ANOINTING

> *"For the grace of God that brings salvation has appeared to all men, teaching us that, denying ungodliness and worldly lusts, we should live soberly, righteously, and godly in the present age."*
> —Titus 2:11–12

Mercy! That last chapter was filled with so many treasures. I feel like we just visited a room filled with wisdom that could guide us for a lifetime. Yet those wisdom ways often come through difficult lessons we learn from the school of hard knocks. The vivid examples from the life of Samson are included in the Bible because they are they are *"useful for teaching, rebuking, correcting and training in righteousness"* (2 Timothy 3:16 NIV). In the body of Christ, past and present, we have had similar tragedies that could have been prevented. They were not the highest will of God. Yet, in His majestic ways, He meshes everything together to design a beautiful tapestry that only the Master Weaver can create. After all, He causes all things to work together for good. (See Romans 8:28.) Right?

In this chapter, we're going to continue to unmask the deception related to the anointing, discover the perils and blessings of weakness, and then receive a revelation of biblical grace so that we can embrace God's blessings and stand strong in the anointing. Another way of saying this is that we are going to discover God's redemptive plan when man mishandles His highly contagious, impacting, and lethal anointing. Or how about, "What to do when 'God-stuff' is too hot to handle!"?

UNMASKING THE DECEPTION

In the previous chapter, we saw how Samson fell into the snare of believing he was an exception to God's standards. Deception will tell you that you are an exception. I call it the "Superman syndrome." A lot of people who are highly gifted fall into this trap. You begin to think you're invincible. Your mailing or subscriber list is bigger than those of others. Your social media platform is greater than theirs and is monetized for ministry. You have more people attending your group, conference, or church than others do. It's easy to begin to think you get away with things because you're better, holier, or smarter than other people or even other spiritual leaders. You can start to believe that you have the Lord's favor because you have the right doctrine or superior revelation.

The bottom line is that you can begin to think that you deserve it, that you earned this anointing and special grace, and thus have a right to special treatment. It's your vindication for all you have overcome! Thoughts from the enemy of self-justification have captured you, and you start to lower your personal standards, even though you preach a higher standard. We must unmask this deception, which usually trips people up in one of three areas: fame, finances, or sexual fascination.

I've mentioned how the anointing can produce notoriety and financial gain that appear to be God's blessing and trick you into believing you're a superhero. The deception found in the fascination and pursuit of sexual pleasure is different, and this deception applies to those who are young, old, male, female, single, married, divorced, or widowed. When you get in the anointing, natural sexual desire can temporarily fade. Your mind is full of godly thoughts, and you feel as if you can conquer the devil. The desires of this world and even hormonal issues and your sex drive can temporarily get put on pause because you are in the anointing. But, in reality, while these desires feel like they are absent, they are actually being stored up. The desire is building and becomes greater after the anointing lifts, after the ministry engagement is completed. This is why moral failures happen in hotel rooms immediately following an evangelistic crusade or when a conference event has come to a close. The enemy understands the nature of the anointing and sets up these ministry-ending encounters ahead of time.

A man or woman of God can also be deceived into believing that these illicit activities are really a service to them. He or she may think, "No one really understands my loneliness, fatigue, and desires, and, as a result, relief is needed." Others warp the truth so they can maneuver around the "rules" and engage in otherwise ungodly behaviors. For example, some Christians believe that having an affair in which intercourse is involved is wrong, but having oral sex is okay. Or some might think having a male attendant waiting at their side to serve in any way desired is okay. After all, it is not adultery. This is deceptive and wrong. The enemy plants these thoughts, and people are seduced. Of course there are spiritual warfare plots against the anointed! This is why we must discern the traps so we can stand strong in the anointing.

So, how can we unmask deception and protect the anointing? John 14:30 gives us the answer; it records Jesus as saying, *"The ruler of this world is coming, and he has nothing in Me."* We protect the anointing when we allow no common ground with the enemy.[12] What does that

---

12. For more on this subject, see chapter 9, "No Common Ground Allowed," in my book *Strike the Mark* (New Kensington, PA: Whitaker House, 2019) and lesson 9 of the corresponding study guide, *Prayers That Strike the Mark* (Franklin, TN: God Encounters Ministries, 2019).

mean? We are not to have anything in common with the enemy—none of his traits or actions.

We must set our boundaries ahead of time. If we do not, the enemy will draw fake lines for us. "Come over here. It's okay. Let's play some games. Who gets to touch whom first?" I know I am being a bit graphic, but this is nothing compared with what really happens. We are to draw lines—make moral decisions ahead of time—and walk in integrity. We are to have nothing in common with the god of this world and his deceitful ways.

The anointing acts in two ways: (1) it covers and protects while you are engaged in ministry, and (2) it exposes your cracks and magnifies your weaknesses. The anointing actually magnifies everything about you. Under the anointing, your giftings are magnified or strengthened, and when the anointing lifts, your defects of character are highlighted. This is why we must be praying as much for the fruit of the Spirit as we are praying for the power and gifts of the Spirit. The apostle Paul admonishes us to both pursue love and earnestly desire spiritual gifts. (See 1 Corinthians 14:1.) Paul pairs up the fruit and the gifts, and so must we.

WHEN THE HAND OF GOD LIFTS

Other people will see cracks in our lives that we don't see. Friends and others in the Lord may issue warnings to us. Years ago, I was given a dream about three things that can occur when the hand of God lifts from a person. You may say, "Well, God will never do that." Yes, He will. He does it as a test. I didn't say He will do it forever, but He will do it temporarily. And we might not even notice. When the hand of God lifts from a man or woman of God, three things happen:

1. The thing that the person has continued to struggle with in private becomes magnified and is sometimes revealed in public.

Whoa. This is why we have to constantly cultivate the fear of the Lord.

2. The thing that the person has feared in the past becomes drawn to them like a magnet, and the enemy camps out, waiting to devour.

3. The desire for former sinful habits, weaknesses, compulsions, and obsessions escalates, and triumphs are now tragedies.

When the hand of the Lord lifts from me, I can turn to entertainment. Now, is that bad? It is not horrible. But I have to be careful not to rely on entertainment for my comfort or for food for my soul.

Before I moved to Tennessee, I was given a stunning dream depicting three reasons for the recent failures of three key spiritual leaders in the heartland of the US. These failures were caused by the exaltation of position, revelation, and doctrine. Let's look at each of these areas.

Exaltation of position. This happens when you are the "king of the mountain." It is when a leader uses their position of authority in a soulish, manipulating manner—pushing or pressuring others to do what they want them to do. Pride sets in, and the spirit of control has a potential place of entrance to exercise its evil domain. Then, "king of the mountain" easily becomes a childish game being played in a fake kingdom sandpile.

Exaltation of revelation. This happens when you exalt your spiritual gift to such an extent that you must continue to display that gift profusely out of a need to be needed. You may have a root of insecurity or rejection. Because I have generational abandonment on one side of my family (my father was kicked out of the home when he was twelve years old), this is something I have had to work through with the Lord. You can fight the exaltation of revelation by finding a meaningful expression of life outside your gift. I have intentionally sowed into interests outside of ministry, which has been helpful.

Exaltation of doctrine. This happens when you elevate personal revelation as being equal to Scripture. You then get yourself isolated in the body of Christ, sometimes through rejection, and you formulate your revelation into an elite doctrine. Let me say this clearly: Jesus is the only Truth. When *a* truth asserts itself as *the* Truth, that truth has just become an error. Just because you are gifted, visit heaven, or have profound visionary experiences doesn't automatically mean you can create new truth and neglect the Truth. A gift is a gift, not a reward for perfect doctrine. You have all the covenant benefits that the Scriptures permit. And those benefits are many! So, stay within those boundaries without elevating personal revelation, and you will succeed.

I want you to be as unique as you're supposed to be in Christ Jesus. I want you to flow powerfully in the anointing of the Holy Spirit, confirming the gospel with signs and wonders all over the world. And I want you to protect the anointing by having discernment to avoid deception. How can you do that? By being grounded in the Word of God, walking in moral integrity, and remaining accountable to those whom God has placed around you for your good.

THE PERILS AND BLESSINGS OF WEAKNESS

Another way we can protect the anointing is by avoiding the perils and embracing the blessings of weakness. People's weaknesses can knock them out for a season, for sure. Some of the most miserable people on earth are those who have operated in the anointing and then walked away from it. Jonah went lower and lower and lower and lower until he praised the Lord at the lowest place in the earth. When he finally yielded and praised God in the belly of a fish, God spoke to the fish, and Jonah got a fresh start to fulfill God's word upon his life. (See Jonah 2:1–3:4.) No matter how low a person goes, there's always redemption.

Weakness has its perils, but it also has its blessings. The apostle Paul wrote, *"When I am weak, then I am strong"* (2 Corinthians 12:10). Huh? I wish God would make up His mind! Yet He did, because He operates as a co-laborer with us. We are weak, but because He is strong, we have strength in our weakness. God chooses to use us for His glory. When He anoints a person, the anointing can develop more rapidly than the character of the individual. As I have repeatedly emphasized, we must take the initiative to grow our character in order to protect our anointing.

Luke 14:28 (NLT) quotes this wisdom from Jesus: *"Don't begin until you count the cost. For who would begin construction of a building without first calculating the cost to see if there is enough money to finish it?"* These are wise words for anyone setting out to minister in any manner—from full-time vocational ministry to volunteering in their local church. We can protect the anointing upon what God wants to build by counting the cost.

Have you noticed that, in our immaturity, we raise our hand and say, "God, I'm ready!" But we're not. We often volunteer out of selfish ambition or, at best, mixed motivation. Then God puts something on our plate, and we cry out, "Lord, I'm not ready!" But we are. In the first instance, we are volunteering with our abilities in mind. In the second instance, we have come to see that we can't do it on our own and are dependent solely upon His ability. This is why Paul said, *"Therefore most gladly I will rather boast in my infirmities, that the power of Christ may rest upon me"* (2 Corinthians 12:9).

In the same way that the process of childhood development and formation can never be sped up, let's allow time for Christian maturation as we become true disciples of Christ. This protects the anointing.

There tend to be two kinds of people or ministries: a shooting star and a North Star. Shooting stars are brilliant people who are here today but burn out quickly and are gone tomorrow. North Stars are those who become steady, fixed lights and, over time, inspire many people through the characteristics of faithfulness. They are among those who daily choose to go for the double, with the fullness of character and the fullness of power.

NEEDED: A REVELATION OF BIBLICAL GRACE

To protect the anointing, in addition to having a proper understanding of our weakness as broken vessels, we need a revelation of biblical grace. God's grace is sufficient (see 2 Corinthians 12:9), and it is only by the grace of God that any of us can stand (see Romans 5:2). Grace is such a wonder!

Titus 2:11–14 offers us some key biblical lessons on grace:

For the grace of God that brings salvation has appeared to all men, teaching us that, denying ungodliness and worldly lusts, we should live soberly, righteously, and godly in the present age, looking for the blessed hope and glorious appearing of our great God and Savior Jesus Christ, who gave Himself for us, that He might redeem us from every lawless deed and purify for Himself His own special people, zealous for good works.

Look at what Titus is saying. Grace teaches us to deny ungodliness and worldly lusts. Grace does not teach licentiousness. That's right. Grace does not teach us conduct that lacks legal or moral restraints. Grace does not teach that it's okay to go get drunk and then prophesy. In the past, there was a church in our region where the members of the youth group would get drunk on their birthdays because their so-called hindrances would diminish, and they would feel the courage to step out and use their supposed gifts. It's true that the walls would come down and revelatory gifts could flow because *"God's gifts and his call are irrevocable"* (Romans 11:29 NIV). Yet things would flow so freely that some would get in a hot tub, and clothes would come off for a topless prophesying party. Michal Ann and I had to rescue a whole bunch of kids from out of the decadence of deception. I'm not exaggerating one bit, and I will not mention other shocking immorality that some Christians are okay with under the umbrella of so-called grace. Hyper-grace doctrines have caused enormous problems globally.

Holy Spirit, deliver us from deception, and empower us to heed the God-breathed words of Titus and live *"soberly, righteously, and godly in the present age."*

I celebrate grace. I love grace. And receiving true teaching about God's grace has been one of the most liberating things that has happened in my life. I am so much freer and so much better because I am a recipient of grace. Let's understand the biblical view of grace so we can protect the precious anointing of the Holy Spirit and fulfill Jesus's call to bring His kingdom everywhere we go.

THE SUSTAINING PRAYER OF JABEZ

Years ago, the prayer of Jabez recorded in 1 Chronicles 4:10 received significant attention around the world. Let's see what this one verse has to say:

> *And Jabez called on the God of Israel saying, "Oh, that You would bless me indeed, and enlarge my territory, that Your hand would be with me, and that You would keep me from evil, that I may not cause pain!" So God granted him what he requested.*

I remember that when the book *The Prayer of Jabez* came out in 2000, some people jumped on the bandwagon right away; they committed the above verse to memory and made it part of their daily prayers. Others wondered if the prayer was biblical enough to pray since it asked God for blessings, and still others began to hear stories about God answering prayers and feared what God might really do.

Am I afraid of a territory being enlarged? Not in the least bit. Am I afraid of increase? Not at all. Am I afraid of being blessed? Nope. Am I afraid of the double? Definitely not! Am I afraid of your having a global ministry of deliverance, driving out demons in Jesus's name, and confirming the gospel with signs and wonders to millions of people? Of course not. Why am I not afraid of any of these things? Because one drop of the blood of Jesus is more powerful than all of the kingdom of darkness. Come on!

The thief will not steal, kill, or destroy the good work the Lord has begun in you. (See John 10:10.) Not through the deception related to the anointing or the exaltation of position, revelation, or doctrine. Not through hero worship. Not through a misunderstanding of grace. You have feet of clay. I have feet of clay. But our feet are on the Rock. We need one another, and when we stay together, we form the "cluster anointing." The new wine is not found in you alone, right? Grapes grow in a cluster, and the new wine of the Spirit forms in the cluster. (See Isaiah 65:8.)

I love the next generation. But God ain't finished with us older folks yet! I've never been hungrier to encounter the glorious Son of God and the blessings He bestows! You think you're going to outrun me? I'm gonna catch my third wind. I do want you to go farther than I. I want to cheer you on and champion you. We are experiencing a great harvest across the earth right now, and we need everyone fully engaged and anointed. I believe that the greatest harvest, which will yield billions of souls, is still coming.

Do you see the purpose of standing strong in the anointing? God does not want this new wine wasted! God does not want another generation to lose their inheritance. God wants us to work together, stand strong, and embrace His blessings of supernatural encounters together. Do your part to bring in the great harvest by protecting the anointing on your life, and share it with others. Remember, in Christ Jesus, we are better together!

PRAYER TO PROTECT THE ANOINTING

In humility, I cry out to You, God, to change my weaknesses into Your strengths. Holy Spirit, reveal practical steps I can take as You conform me into the image of Christ. Lead me to the Rock of my salvation, where all things are steadfast and immovable in Him! Jesus, I know You love me with an everlasting love. Thank You for Your mercy. I want to have strong character to protect the anointing and carry the gifts You have given to me. I ask that the fear of the Lord would be my treasure and a fragrance around my life. Bring me out of any fog of deception in the mishandling of the anointing so I can faithfully handle Your power. Help me to grow in wisdom and in favor and stature with God and man. Keep me from stumbling so that I can stand in the presence of Your glory, blameless and with great joy. Guide my steps to walk in the straight and narrow way. I will continue in Your Word so that I can know the Truth that sets me free. Thank You, Jesus, that Your grace is sufficient for me. Amen and amen.

PART TWO

INTERPRETING THE WAYS OF THE SPIRIT

6

THE DIVERSITY OF SUPERNATURAL ENCOUNTERS

*"To each is given the manifestation of the
Spirit for the common good."*
—1 Corinthians 12:7 (ESV)

My four married children have blessed me with twelve grandchildren to date. Children see the world through creative eyes and are constantly asking questions. I was like that as a child. My mom often told me, "You were the most curious child that I had. You were always asking questions." I wonder if curiosity has anything to do with our relationship with God or the relationship that we can have with the Holy Spirit today. I think so. Adults can get overwhelmed by all the questions that get thrown at them, but God loves them! When we approach God with a humble, teachable heart, we are able to see more clearly the diverse creativity of the Holy Spirit.

Even if you feel that you are already familiar with various types of supernatural encounters, I encourage you to join me in examining this subject with a childlike heart. I didn't say child*ish*, I said child*like*, because the Bible teaches that only those who have a childlike heart can truly enter and enjoy the kingdom of God. Understanding the different types of supernatural encounters that we or others can experience helps us to embrace these blessings when God releases them. It also provides us with wisdom to steward them as we stand strong in the anointing. (We will further investigate the wisdom ways of the anointing in part 3 of this book.)

The Holy Spirit has so much for us! These supernatural gifts are like gold coins that Jesus entrusts to us to invest and multiply for a return in the kingdom of God. (See Luke 19:11–27.) Don't hide them. It's time to embrace these wonderful manifestations of God's presence that display His greatness and lead people to Jesus!

THE CREATIVE HOLY SPIRIT AT WORK

The Holy Spirit creates an endless variety of gifts, ministries, and operations within the body of Christ. Let's look at some of them through the writings of Paul the apostle, who greatly expanded our understanding of this spiritual reality in his first letter to the Corinthian church:

Gifts. Paul said, *"Now there are varieties of gifts, but the same Spirit"* (1 Corinthians 12:4 ESV, NASB, NASB95). Most translations use the word *"gifts"* in this verse, so I want to point out the word *"varieties"* here, which is translated as *"diversities"* in the King James Version (KJV) and the *New King James Version* (NKJV). The *New International Version* (NIV) uses the phrase *"different kinds"* of gifts. *The Passion Translation* (TPT) renders this verse as follows: *"It is the same Holy Spirit who continues to distribute many different varieties of gifts."* This verse is communicating the opposite of uniformity. I so enjoy the creativity of the Holy Spirit, who distributes these grace (Greek, *charis*) gifts in diverse packages for us to use.

Ministries. Paul continues, "*And there are varieties of ministries, and the same Lord*" (1 Corinthians 12:5 NASB, NASB95). The ESV and NIV use the word *"service."* The KJV translates this word as *"administrations."* Imagine that. The Holy Spirit functions in an administrative capacity. *The Passion Translation* presents the following: "*The Lord Yahweh is one, and he is the one who apportions to believers different varieties of ministries.*"

Let's not become overly familiar with this verse and miss what it says. There are *varieties* of ministries, service, or administrations, whichever word we want to use. There is a diversity of spiritual gifts for the purpose of service. There are a variety of services, but the *same* Lord. When these gifts are brought together, they create a cluster anointing that becomes a ministry that is a service to others.

Operations. Paul continues, "*And there are diversities of operations*" (1 Corinthians 12:6 KJV). The entire verse in the ESV reads, "*And there are varieties of activities, but it is the same God who empowers them all in everyone.*" The NIV uses the phrase "*different kinds of working.*" The NASB and NASB95 use a term I love: "*effects.*" *The Passion Translation* renders this verse as follows: "*The same God distributes different kinds of miracles that accomplish different results through each believer's gift and ministry as he energizes and activates them.*" That covers the subject well!

Now note this: Verse 4 reads, "*The same Spirit.*" Verse 5 reads, "*The same Lord,*" referring to the Lord Jesus. And verse 6 says, "*The same God.*" It sounds like the Trinity is at work. What is exciting to me is that the Godhead is fully involved in the creative process and distribution of these supernatural gift encounters that release divine encounters for others:

- Variety of gifts—same Holy Spirit.
- Variety of ministries, service, administrations—same Lord Jesus Christ.

- Variety of operations, activities, working, or results—same God the Father.

Thank You, Father, Son, and Spirit, for working through gifts, through service, and through an operating empowerment that produces activity of creative diversity. We love You!

How beautiful that the body of Christ is so diverse, and that ministries can be made up of a collection of gifts. Thank God we have to be dependent upon others as we interlock like pieces of a puzzle working together. "Oh, you mean we are actually meant to work together?" Yes! This wide variety of gifts, expressed through different personalities, is further varied by the surrounding circumstances and culture. People don't worship and minister in Nigeria in the same way that they do in Egypt. They don't do these things in India in the same way that they do them in Brazil.

We must move past "vanilla Christianity." The church is supposed to look more like a banana split. On top of the ice cream, you slice up a banana and add some strawberries with a bit (or a bunch!) of chocolate sauce. Maybe some caramel too. You toss on some sprinkles, maybe some peanuts—a little bit of this, a little bit of that. Don't forget a cherry! The body of Christ is colorful and has flavorful expression.

Some of us trip up over cultural differences. If you're going to get tripped up over our diversity here on earth, you're going to struggle when you get to heaven. There is *one* creative God with *many* diverse expressions. Let's expect Him to use us in a variety of ways as we are under His anointing, and then let us anticipate supernatural gift encounters to follow. This posture will lead to many blessings as we stand strong in the anointing.

SIGNS WILL FOLLOW: SPIRITUAL GIFT ENCOUNTERS

Mark 16:17 declares that signs will follow those who believe. As we walk with Jesus, I wonder if we should peek over our shoulders to make sure signs are tagging along. The entire ministry of Jesus confirmed that He was the Messiah through the signs that followed that ministry, and He wants to confirm His Word with signs through us today.

God ordained that the gospel of the kingdom should be preached with signs following. Mark 16:15–20 and other passages in the New Testament show that such encounters characterized the ministry of the early church. We see Philip casting out unclean spirits and healing the sick (see Acts 8:5–7), Paul having no ill effects after a poisonous snake bites his hand, and then an entire island receiving healing through the hands of Paul (see Acts 28:1–10).

Paul told the Roman church that he led the Gentiles to obey God not only through his words but also *"by the power of signs and wonders, through the power of the Spirit of God. So from Jerusalem all the way around to Illyricum, I have fully proclaimed the gospel of Christ"* (Romans 15:19 niv). The gospel of Jesus Christ being fully proclaimed includes signs that follow our faith in Jesus.

I love how the writer of Hebrews calls the salvation we have received "great" (Hebrews 2:3). This passage proclaims, *"This salvation, which was first announced by the Lord, was confirmed to us by those who heard him. God also testified to it by signs, wonders and various miracles, and by gifts of the Holy Spirit distributed according to his will"* (verses 3–4 niv). Let's not miss the end of this verse. Signs include not only what we may consider big things like raising the dead, healing the sick, and driving out demons but also the supernatural gifts of the Holy Spirit. God wants the gospel confirmed by Holy Spirit gifts that are distributed. People can encounter Jesus through you as you flow in the anointing and use your spiritual gifts.

If you're new to the Bible, you may not know that there is no Acts 29. Our record of The Acts of the Apostles stops at chapter 28. But that does not mean that the acts of the Spirit ceased or are supposed to end.

You are to continue those acts of the Spirit. *You* are Acts 29. You are to live out your version of Romans 15 and Hebrews 2.

In our lifetimes, we all can expect to see unprecedented, brilliant displays of God's grace and supernatural power through His gifted people. We will overcome this temporary present darkness as we walk in the kingdom authority of the message of the Lord Jesus Christ. The most effective people aren't always the ones with a big platform—physical or digital. Some of the most effective people are those who carry a towel on their arm, humbly serving Christ by ministering to *"the least of these"* in the "highways and byways," inviting to the marriage supper of the Lamb all who will come. (See Matthew 22:9–11; 25:40–45.)

I want every believer to be aware of and equipped to use the supernatural gifts of the Spirit to help others encounter the love of God. For the rest of this chapter, I lay a biblical foundation of what these diverse gifts are. I trust it will whet your appetite for more of the Holy Spirit! But what follows will only give you a taste of what is possible because I have written in detail on the supernatural gifts of the Spirit in other books. Please reference the footnotes in this chapter for specific books that will help you go deeper.

Sometimes people see only nine spiritual gifts mentioned in the Bible, specifically those listed in 1 Corinthians 12. There are, however, at least twenty spiritual gifts recorded in Scripture.[13] The list of nine in 1 Corinthians 12 includes spiritual gifts that I divide into three categories: revelatory gifts, power gifts, and vocal gifts.

The gifts of the Spirit are like a rainbow, in which there is no clear demarcation where one color begins and another color ends. Rather, the shades overlap. The gifts are the same way. They are not to be dissected so precisely, like you would dissect a dead specimen. In my growing-up years, I wanted to be a NASA research biologist. I even boldly declared

---

13. See chapter 2, "What Are the Spiritual Gifts?" in my book *Releasing Spiritual Gifts Today*, in which I list every place in the Bible where a spiritual gift is mentioned.

in front of my entire school assembly that I would be the head biologist at the NASA research and development center. While I didn't land there occupationally, my analytical mind loves to dissect things. We, however, can tend to overly dissect spiritual gifts. I prefer to organize these specific nine living gifts by putting them in clusters of three. I love the richness of supernatural diversity that comes through anointed vessels and helps us and others to encounter the living Christ.

CLUSTERS OF SPIRITUAL GIFTS IN 1 CORINTHIANS 12

REVELATORY GIFTS: GIFTS THAT REVEAL

Revelatory gifts are gifts that reveal, and we can find three of them in 1 Corinthians 12: a word of wisdom, a word of knowledge, and a gift of discerning of spirits. *"For to one is given the word of wisdom through the Spirit, to another the word of knowledge through the same Spirit,…to another discerning of spirits"* (verses 8, 10).

Notice that Paul says that there are *"spirits."* Why is *spirits* plural? Because there is the Holy Spirit, there are angelic spirits, there are demonic spirits, and there's the human spirit. A person with this revelatory grace gift can peer into, perceive, distinguish, and differentiate between them. They can know and see the shades of gray and perceive the motivating spirit that's behind an operation.

I shared that gifts often overlap, and the word of knowledge and word of wisdom can energize other gifts into action. The Holy Spirit will give you a literal word that provides knowledge or wisdom you did not have previously. The word of knowledge or wisdom is supernatural in itself. The Creator of the universe has just given you private information you did not have previously. That's beyond the natural. What is exciting is that, if you step out in faith to deliver the word under the anointing of the Spirit, the word can release additional supernatural activity.

POWER GIFTS: GIFTS THAT DO

The power gifts are gifts that get stuff done: *"To another faith by the same Spirit, to another gifts of healings by the same Spirit, to another the working of miracles"* (1 Corinthians 12:9–10). We can again see how the gifts overlap. The gift of faith—which is different from having faith in Jesus for salvation—helps you tune in to the Holy Spirit to receive a word of knowledge or wisdom. The gift of faith then prompts you that healings and miracles are possible—not just theoretically but right now!

In 1 Corinthians 12:9, we find one of the few instances in the Bible where the word *gift* is plural. Paul instructs us that there are *"gifts of healings."* This is a connotation of the Greek word *therapeuo*, which refers to therapies. I believe God has expansive varieties of anointings to be released in His therapeutic manner for "natural-supernatural" healing. What is natural-supernatural? If David could play a harp so that a demon would lift from Saul (see 1 Samuel 16:14–23), you know what that is? Anointed music *therapeuo*—music therapy under the anointing of the Holy Spirit.

God wants you to know that He will use every tool in the tool chest. God wants to use every art form there is. He wants to use music. He wants to use visual arts. He wants to use *listening*. Did you know that listening is one of the greatest healing gifts there is? Let's not become so familiar with the laying on of hands to heal the sick that we minimize the supernatural capacity to listen, which can release supernatural healing. Does that stretch you?

If you are familiar with my history, you know that, at one time, my late wife, Michal Ann, and I could not have children. I was the senior pastor at Harvest Fellowship in Warrensburg, Missouri, and we had reached out for prayer from everyone we could. The who's who of the charismatic movement had prayed for us, and it seemed like nothing happened. But sometimes another prayer tips the scales. Do I always understand all these supernatural ways? No, but the Bible doesn't say,

"Understand it with your mind." Proverbs 3:5–6 declares, *"Trust in the* LORD *with all your heart, and lean not on your own understanding; in all your ways acknowledge Him, and He shall direct your paths."*

As the senior pastor, I had invited Mahesh Chavda to speak and minister. At the end of the service, he released a word of knowledge that said, "There's someone here who is barren, and God wants to heal them." Well, everybody there knew that we couldn't have kids, and we had already been prayed for by anyone and everyone. I thought, "This word can't be for us because everybody knows this information already." But I felt an elbow nudge from both Michal Ann and the Holy Spirit. Along with that nudge came therapeutic thoughts like, "It's time to get over the feeling of shame, the embarrassment, your pride. Get over the familiarity, get over the disappointment." I resolved in my heart, "We're trying again."

Here Michal Ann and I were, up on platform, and Mahesh looked away from us. (You might notice that prophetic people sometimes look somewhere else. They don't tend to look right at you.) Then he looked above Michal Ann's head and said, "Oh, I see you as a joyous mother of three children." You can imagine our response. We were just trying to believe for one child! We both fell to the floor. Did we faint because he had said *three?* Michal Ann told me that a warmth went into her midsection, and, for four mornings in a row after we received prayer, this same warmth would come upon her in the mornings. She said it was as if a spiritual anesthesia would come upon her, and then a pulling and a stretching would happen in her midsection.

God did what only He could do because it had been medically documented that it was impossible for us to have children. A few days after Christmas that year, Michal Ann came down with some strong flulike symptoms. I prayed for her, but things just got worse. So I took her to our primary care doctor. He came back into the room and gave us the news that this sickness was not going to leave for a long time. He then proceeded to tell us the good news that we were expecting. Yes, just as the Lord had given me a dream in the first year of our marriage, we were to have a son! I want you to know that *"Jesus Christ is the same yesterday, today, and forever"* (Hebrews 13:8). We ended up with *four* miracle kids (Mahesh only saw to the point where we had three children), and, as I wrote at the beginning of this chapter, my children have blessed me so far with twelve grandchildren.

Can you see how a cluster of supernatural gifts came together to release this miracle? It involved prayers from many people, the gift of faith, Mahesh giving a word of knowledge and our responding in faith, gifts of healings, and the working of miracles. A beautiful rainbow forms as the spiritual gifts work together to create something extraordinary that glorifies Jesus and reminds us that God's promise of healing is for us today.

Michal Ann has lived in heaven for over sixteen years now. She never got to participate in any of our kids' weddings or see our grandchildren. But at one Christmas celebration in my home in recent years, while unwrapping presents, I looked at Justin, our oldest son, and the Holy Spirit said, "Within every miracle is the God DNA of multiplication." Then I realized that everyone in that room was a miracle that came from the seed of faith. I was also keenly aware that Michal Ann was in the *"great...cloud of witnesses"* (Hebrews 12:1), and she knew what was going on that very day.

Who in the natural is going to believe that a barren couple can have children? Barren means barren. But not to God, and not to the person who will stand strong in the anointing to release the supernatural gifts of the Spirit.

VOCAL GIFTS: GIFTS THAT SPEAK

The last cluster of three—the vocal gifts—speak life-giving words. The second half of 1 Corinthians 12:10 completes the list: *"To another prophecy,...to another different kinds of tongues, to another the interpretation of tongues."* The misunderstanding and misuse of these gifts, specifically, have caused a great deal of disruption in the church. The apostle Paul must have seen some of the same issues because he interjected an entire section on love into his letter. Couples often hear words from 1 Corinthians 13—the "Love Chapter"—at their wedding. Paul called this *"a more excellent way"* (1 Corinthians 12:31): using the supernatural gifts of the Spirit *with love.*

First Corinthians 14 then begins with, *"Pursue love, and desire spiritual gifts, but especially that you may prophesy"* (verse 1). Did you see the word *"and"* in that verse? Again, we are to love others *and* desire spiritual gifts, especially prophecy. Why? Because prophecy *"speaks edification and exhortation and comfort"* to people (verse 3). These gifts must have needed even more explanation because Paul continued to describe how to use them. (See verses 4–33.) Paul wanted us to avoid the traps and embrace the blessings of these supernatural gifts.

I encourage you to read my book *Releasing Spiritual Gifts Today* and my various books on the prophetic for additional teaching. Again, my purpose in this book is not necessarily to explain the gifts in detail but to encourage you to *use* them and to use them *wisely* in the anointing so you can partner with the intent for which the Holy Spirit gives them: to point people to Jesus and encourage them in their personal faith.

Because Paul wrote more extensively on the topic of tongues, let me share a personal story about this gift. I explained in an earlier chapter how the Holy Spirit led me to pray in one form of the gift of tongues—a private personal prayer tongue—for two hours at a time, which I did as a spiritual discipline. But then, after I had spent that time of preparation before the Lord, the Holy Spirit orchestrated a time in Guatemala when I supernaturally spoke publicly in a known human language, yet one that I did not know and had never studied.

During a World Congress on Evangelism, while I was speaking in front of more than ten thousand leaders from around Latin America and the world, the Holy Spirit said, "Begin to speak in tongues out loud." I felt the anointing come upon me as I started to speak in "different kinds of tongues," which ended up including a known human language and dialect that did not require interpretation.

I was told that I spoke a little in Korean, but mostly in Ixil, the Mayan language of a Guatemalan tribe. About a hundred and twenty short Ixil people moved to the front of grand the auditorium after they heard me declare in their dialect, "The door is open. The door is open. The door is open. Come for yourself because the door of the kingdom of God has been opened for you. The door is open. The door is open." They came running to the front dressed in the patterned clothes of their tribe. I stepped down from the platform and went among them with the anointing upon me as the wind of God came blowing upon them, empowering them with the Holy Spirit. That evening, we all experienced something like what happened in Acts 2. How kind of the Holy Spirit to release this supernatural gift so that a tribe of people could hear such a personal invitation. What a loving God we have!

VISIONARY ENCOUNTERS[14]

Both Scripture and Christian history display the occurrence of a great diversity of visionary encounters. Should we be surprised at this? John 5:19 records Jesus sharing a secret to the effectiveness of His ministry: *"Most assuredly, I say to you, the Son can do nothing of Himself, but what He sees the Father do; for whatever He does, the Son also does in like manner."* I love that Jesus said, *"Most assuredly...."* Jesus wanted us to emphatically know that He literally perceived and saw His Father in action and did the same things His Father did. We are called into this interactive natural-supernatural relationship with our Father as well.

---

14. My book *The Seer* (Shippensburg, PA: Destiny Image, 2012) and its corresponding curriculum kit are excellent resources from which to learn more about this topic.

As if Jesus wanted to make sure His followers understood a major way in which He received His guidance, He continued, *"For the Father loves the Son, and shows Him all things that He Himself does"* (verse 20).

What are some of the supernatural ways through which the Father shows us His will? Let's take a look together:

- Spiritual perception or a feeling we experience
- A pictorial vision, like a snapshot that comes internally or externally
- A panoramic vision that moves like a motion picture
- A vision with our eyes wide open
- A vision with our eyes shut
- Overlays of images
- Many other expressions

Numbers 12:6 tells us, *"If there is a prophet among you, I, the Lord, make Myself known to him in a vision; I speak to him in a dream."* There are about three hundred verses in the Bible that talk about how God speaks in visions and dreams. These avenues are actually a primary way through which God has communicated with people, as recorded in Scripture.

A trance is another form of visionary encounter. "Wow," you may say, "that's getting a little intense." But a trance is actually not that intense when you study what it means. The Greek word translated as *"trance"* in the book of Acts (see, for example, Acts 10:10; 11:5) is *ekstasis*, from which the English word *ecstasy* is derived, so a trance is an ecstatic state in the Spirit. It just means that your human volition is temporarily put on pause so that you are caught up in such a manner that you receive only those things that the Holy Spirit intends.[15]

The same Greek word is used in Mark 16, which describes the astonishment of the women at the empty tomb after they saw an angel who told them Jesus had been resurrected: *"And they went out and fled from the tomb, for trembling and astonishment [ekstasis] had gripped them"* (verse 8 NASB, NASB95). Some other examples of trances in the Bible include the following:

- In Revelation 1:17, John wrote that when he saw Jesus in a vision, he *"fell at His feet as dead."*

- In Daniel 10:9, Daniel wrote this about his great vision: *"While I heard the sound of his words I was in a deep sleep on my face, with my face to the ground."*

- Ezekiel 1 describes *"the hand of the LORD"* (verse 3) that came upon Ezekiel and brought him into a state of being in which he was able to receive visions of God.

- Acts 22:17 (ESV) is most clear about this state, as Paul testified, *"When I had returned to Jerusalem"*—and here's the key—*"and was praying in the temple, I fell into a trance."*

Supernatural visionary encounters still happen today. Perhaps you've heard of Muslims encountering Jesus as the "Man in white." One man claimed that this Man in white visited him every night for a month, asking him to write down what He said. A Middle Eastern missionary stated, "God is moving inside the Middle East with dreams, visions, and personal visitations."[16]

---

15. Please see my book *The Seer* for detailed teaching on the subject of trances.
16. Mark Ellis, "'Man in White' Appears to Muslims, Brings Salvation," God Reports, May 12, 2022, https://www.godreports.com/2022/05/man-in-white-appears-to-muslims-brings-salvation/.

Dreams are sleeping visions that everyone encounters. You may not always remember your dreams, but everyone has dreams, and God speaks through them. I've found roughly twelve categories of dreams, including dreams of destiny, edification, exhortation, comfort, correction, direction, instruction, impartation, spiritual warfare, and more. Dreams can carry a tangible presence of God and require some diligence to understand since they are often parabolic. My books *The Scribe* and *Dream Language* will help you with some practical tools to journal your dreams and discover what God is saying to you as you rest.[17]

Job 33:14–16 (NLT) declares, *"For God speaks again and again, though people do not recognize it. He speaks in dreams, in visions of the night, when deep sleep falls on people as they lie in their beds. He whispers in their ears and terrifies them with warnings."*

And if that weren't enough, the Bible contains accounts of heavenly visitations and actual heavenly experiences. Some examples include the following:

- Enoch walked with God and did not die because *"God took him"* (Genesis 5:24).

- Moses encountered God on Mount Sinai and also talked with God *"face to face."* (See Exodus 19; 33:11.)

- It is believed that Paul was caught up into the third heaven. (See 2 Corinthians 12:2.)

It's important to see that the apostle Paul does not treat these amazing supernatural encounters with overfamiliarity. They are not another notch on his belt. Notice how he handles these precious experiences. Instead of saying, "Hey, listen, guys, I just had this awesome encounter," he speaks in the third person about *"a man"* who *"was caught up to the third heaven. Whether it was in the body or out of the body I do*

---

17. See James W. Goll, *The Scribe* (Shippensburg, PA: Destiny Image, 2020) and James W. Goll and Michal Ann Goll, *Dream Language* (Shippensburg, PA: Destiny Image, 2006).

not know—God knows. And I know that this man—whether in the body or apart from the body I do not know, but God knows—was caught up to paradise and heard inexpressible things" (2 Corinthians 12:2–4 NIV). We can follow what Paul modeled for us and handle these experiences with humility and the fear of the Lord.

OPEN HEAVENS AND BEYOND

The Bible is full of verses that say that *"the heavens were opened"* (Ezekiel 1:1; Matthew 3:16) or include similar expressions or concepts. An open heaven is a vision where there appears to be a hole or an opening that occurs in the sky, in the celestial realm. Heavenly sights of God and of those who dwell in the heavenlies become seeable; the unseen becomes accessible.

I know this may sound like the start of a science-fiction book, but we are not alone! I've gleaned from more than a hundred and ten books and have spent over thirty years researching the subject of angels and angelic encounters. A few biblical examples of actual appearances of angels include the following:

- Jacob saw an angel and literally wrestled with him. (See Genesis 32:24–31.)

- Joshua saw Jesus as the Commander of the Lord's Army. (See Joshua 5:13–15.)

- An angel of the Lord appeared to Zacharias as he ministered in the temple. (See Luke 1:8–11.)

- An angel appeared to the centurion Cornelius with a message from God. (See Acts 10:1–7.)

My late wife and I have encountered angels, and possibly you have too—maybe even when you were unaware of it. (See Hebrews 13:2 KJV.) Angelic encounters are for today.[18]

STANDING STRONG IN DIVERSE SUPERNATURAL ENCOUNTERS

Standing strong in the anointing requires that we know God—the God of the Bible. This God is alive and wants to interact with us through supernatural encounters like spiritual gift encounters, visionary encounters, angelic encounters, heavenly encounters, and, of course, God encounters. When the Holy Spirit releases His anointed presence, and the supernatural breaks out, what will you do? I'll share again what the Holy Spirit said to me: "If you can't jump in the middle of it, bless it. If you can't bless it, gently observe it. But if you can't simply observe it, then just don't criticize what you don't understand."

In part 3 of this book, we'll look more closely at how to walk wisely through supernatural experiences because there are traps to avoid. But, for now, my goal has been to say, "Hey! God wants to encounter you, and He wants to encounter others through you!" While there are traps to avoid, there are many more blessings to enjoy!

PRAYER TO GROW IN DIVERSE SUPERNATURAL ENCOUNTERS

Gracious Father, in the wonderful name of Jesus, I hunger for more diverse supernatural encounters in my life. I declare that the Holy Spirit, who was creative at the beginning of the world, is the same today and forever in His divine nature. Therefore, I say, "Come, Holy Spirit, and be creative in my life!" Release a diversity of spiritual gift encounters for me, Your child. As You explain in James 4:2, I do not have because I do not ask—so I ask! Send more, Lord! I welcome every form of visionary

---

18. For further study on these topics, see these resources by James W. Goll and Michal Ann Goll: *Angelic Encounters* (Lake Mary, FL: Charisma House, 2004), *Angelic Encounters Today Study Guide* (Franklin, TN: Creative Productions, 2013), and *God Encounters Today* (Shippensburg, PA: Destiny Image, 2017).

encounter as well. Release an increase of dreams, visions, and visitations, in Jesus's name! I align myself with the completed work of the cross of Calvary and expect that supernatural encounters will be on the rise in my life, for the glory of God. Amen and amen!

7

UNDERSTANDING PROPHETIC ACTIONS

"For if we are beside ourselves, it is for God;
or if we are of sound mind, it is for you."
—2 Corinthians 5:13

How exciting it can be when the heightened manifest presence of the Holy Spirit comes and supernatural encounters happen. What occurs can also be confusing. What in the world should you do when you see or hear about manifestations such as shaking, trembling, stomping, being frozen in position, staggering, falling, heavy breathing, fluttering eyes, stammering lips, sensations of tingling, oil being secreted from the hands, running in place, weeping, laughing, shouting, stillness, trances, resting, feelings of heat or fire on the body, groaning, roaring, or travailing? And those are just a few that I've seen. There are more! What is really going on anyway?

To stand strong in the anointing when mysterious and sometimes wacky things happen means to avoid certain things and embrace others. For example, scoffing at what looks silly and making assumptions about the person manifesting the action is not helpful. But asking the Holy Spirit for insight and loving the person through their experience pleases the Lord.

So, in this chapter we're going to get into the details of this narrow but important topic of understanding prophetic actions. Some of this content may stretch you, and some of it will bring some sanity. Let's learn how to discern the prophetic actions that occur when people encounter the supernatural.

PROPHETIC GESTURES IN COMMUNICATION

In December 1994, I was ministering in England during a time when dramatic and visible supernatural physical manifestations were occurring. The "Toronto Blessing," a term used by the British media to describe what was happening at what was then called the Toronto Airport Vineyard Church, had started in January of that year. Many Christians had never seen such animated physical responses to the presence of God, and people were wondering if these responses were biblical or heretical.

Eleven months later, I was in England speaking at some meetings where the anointing was strong and this phenomenon was breaking out. Amid what appeared to be chaos, the Holy Spirit spoke clearly to me, "Preach the gospel." I was given the understanding at the time that this was what it was like on the day of Pentecost described in Acts 2. The Bible says that the people *were all amazed and perplexed, saying to one another, 'Whatever could this mean?'* (Acts 2:12). As I looked over what was happening, I asked the Holy Spirit, "How in the world do I keep my focus and preach the gospel in the midst of these manifestations?" The next thought came from the Holy Spirit: "The purpose of this refreshing is to reveal the person of Jesus Christ."

That was a mic-drop moment. As we go through this chapter, and as we experience these supernatural encounters, let's keep this principle in front of us: these dimensions of prophetic gestures and actions must ultimately reveal the person of the Lord Jesus Christ and direct others to Him. There you go.

With that as our foundation and aim, let's dive in and look more closely at these gestures in communication. Some categories of these actions include the following:

- An impartation from God for empowering in the Spirit
- A form of intercession to God for intervention
- Worship of God as a form of nonverbal communication
- Prophetic proclamations to people, nations, and even geographical areas through actions
- A dimension of personal ministry to people in need, breaking off realms of darkness by releasing the power of the Holy Spirit
- A discerning of a demonic assignment where the gift of discerning of spirits determines the root of an issue[19]
- An activity that originates with the Holy Spirit but is then amplified by man's additives. Again, God does not need man's help!

These prophetic gestures are acts or actions that communicate thoughts. Romans 12:1 (NIV) tells us, "*Offer your bodies as a living sacrifice, holy and pleasing to God—this is your true and proper worship.*" We

---

19. For more on this subject, see the books and curriculum kits for *Deliverance from Darkness* (Grand Rapids, MI: Chosen, 2010), *The Discerner* (New Kensington, PA: Whitaker House, 2017), and *Releasing Spiritual Gifts Today*.

don't love Jesus only with our hearts. Jesus said to *"love the* LORD *your God with all your heart, all your soul, all your mind, and all your strength"* (Mark 12:30 NLT). Gestures can be used as a "prophetic mouthpiece" of God on the earth, releasing an expression of the heart of God to both the believing community and the unbelieving community.

These gestures can be either spontaneous or planned demonstrative actions. They may release a message and/or an activity of the power and presence of God. They are manifestations or expressions of, and to, the Holy Spirit. My friend and former ministry colleague Michael Sullivant wrote:

> The Hebrew and biblical model of the unity of personality implies that the spirit affects the body. At times the human spirit is so affected by the glory of God, the human body is not capable of containing the intensity of these spiritual encounters and strange physical behavior results. Sometimes, though certainly not always, the bodily responses are human responses to the spirit's activity and not directly caused by the Holy Spirit. However, this does not imply that they are therefore carnal and should be forbidden.[20]

So, what are these supernatural phenomena for?

1. *To signal God's presence.* Certain shaking motions may precede a prophetic utterance. Some shaking activities may demonstrate empowerment. Still other bodily movements may indicate a demonic presence. A collision of light and darkness might have just occurred.

2. *To wake us up.* God is shaking us to wake us up! Ephesians 5:14 (NIV) states, *"Wake up, sleeper, rise from the dead, and Christ will*

---

20. Michael Sullivant and Mike Bickle, *God's Manifest Presence: Understanding the Phenomena That Accompany the Spirit's Ministry* (United States: Metro Vineyard Fellowship, 1995).

shine on you." This command precedes the exhortation to be filled continually with the Holy Spirit. We are to wake up and seek to be continually filled with the wine of God's Spirit. If we haven't heeded God's previous wake-up calls, perhaps He is now shaking us to awaken us and get our attention.

3. *To humble us.* When Randy Clark, founder of Global Awakening, asked God why He was bringing all those phenomena with the Toronto Blessing, God replied that He was looking for people who were willing to publicly look foolish for the honor of His name. Paul Cain, the seer-prophet, was known for saying, "God offends the mind to reveal the heart." The bottom-line issue is one of control. Will we surrender to the ways of the Holy Spirit when He comes in power?

4. *To anoint for empowerment.* Our being filled with the Holy Spirit is a repeatable experience, and it is one that we are commanded to continually have. (See Ephesians 5:18.) God will sovereignly move on us to impart supernatural ability to do certain things. A new commissioning requires a new empowering. This is why Paul states in 2 Timothy 1:6 (NIV), *"I remind you to fan into flame the gift of God, which is in you through the laying on of my hands."* Possibly, you've seen people moving their hands to "fan" another person, as if to fan into flame the anointing that is coming on that individual to empower them for ministry.

5. *To point the way.* A road sign only points to a destination; it is not the destination itself. In the same way, supernatural phenomena are only signs. Our destiny is to become conformed to the image of Christ. (See Romans 8:29.) When the Holy Spirit comes in power, He comes to make us like Jesus, to heal us and to empower us to stand strong so we will fulfill our roles in His mission.

THE BATTLE BETWEEN EXTRAVAGANCE AND RESPECTABILITY[21]

In the Scriptures, in the war between extravagance and respectability, God always judges respectability, and He exonerates, or justifies, extravagance. The anointing of the Holy Spirit brings about the supernatural—something beyond the natural, something extra. We can see many examples in Scripture where people expressed themselves in a way that is "extra."

Shortly before Jesus was crucified, He spent some time with His friends Mary, Martha, and Lazarus. Mary took a jar of expensive, fragrant oil and anointed Jesus's feet. (See, for example, Mark 14:3–9; John 12:1–7.) This expression of love was worth one year's salary and was a blessing to Jesus, but those around Jesus saw Mary's expression as something bad: *"Why was this fragrant oil wasted?"* they said. *"For it might have been sold…and given to the poor"* (Mark 14:4). Feeding the poor was a biblical, respectable activity. Jesus, however, blessed the act of extravagance. Similarly, I believe the Holy Spirit wants to pour out His anointing upon people in such a way that there is an extravagant expression.

Second Samuel 6:14–22 tells of the time when David danced wildly before the ark of the Lord wearing a priestly linen garment rather than his royal robes. Michal, his wife, rebuked him for not being respectable. God blessed David for his extravagance; Michal, the one who esteemed respectability, was, on the other hand, cursed by God with barrenness.

The one hundred and twenty believers who gathered in the upper room on the day of Pentecost were accused of drunkenness because of their demonstrative display of the Spirit. Yet Peter proclaimed that the supernatural conduct pointed to fulfilled prophecy, not the misuse of alcohol. (See Acts 2:1–21.)

Are there traps to avoid in supernatural encounters? Yes, that's why I am writing this book. Is it possible to be deceived? Yes, but our protection

---

21. I have gleaned some of the material in this section from Steve Meeks, prophetic elder at Calvary Community Church in Houston, Texas.

and ability to stand strong in the anointing are rooted in our intimacy with Jesus, not in a fear of being deceived. Some people will say, "But some of this stuff is not in the Bible." The Bible must not be treated only like a rule book. Things not forbidden in Scripture may be allowed when God is initiating them.

The evangelical church today seems only to see the first-century church and the twenty-first-century church. Unfortunately, we tend to have amnesia when it comes to church history. We act like God has done nothing, taught nothing, and showed us nothing in two thousand years. Church history teaches us wisdom, reveals God's activity, and instructs us in His ways: there have been diverse manifestations and the empowering presence of the Holy Spirit in both evangelical and holiness revival movements.[22]

Now, please note: a train needs two tracks on which to run. We are not to make the precious and unusual the only train track there is. There is also the track of natural, mundane spiritual disciplines that we all must maintain. We need both of these tracks. At times, one of the ways of God is offensive to one camp, and the diverse opposite is offensive to the other camp.

Why does God do it in this way? He often offends us, tests us, and humbles us. He knows what He is doing: delivering us and empowering us to ultimately live and act more like Jesus. The fruit of a person's life will always reveal the ultimate outcome of an encounter. I've interviewed many people who were dramatically impacted by the Spirit, and they are different today because of God's presence, power, and love. Jesus wants to capture us and transform us for His glory.

---

22. A helpful summary of supernatural manifestations in revival movements across the church and around the world—including in the evangelical church, not just in the charismatic/Pentecostal church—can be found in Paul L. King, DMin, DTh, "Supernatural Manifestations in Revival History," a paper presented at the 32nd Society of Pentecostal Studies/Wesleyan Theological Society, Joint Conference, March 21, 2003, posted by Ephesians Four Network of Churches & Ministers, June 28, 2018, https://www.ephesiansfour.net/supernatural-manifestations-in-revival-history/.

SYMBOLIC ACTS OF THE PROPHET

Old Testament prophets did some pretty crazy stuff in obedience to God to release what He wanted to say to Israel. In his book *Developing the Prophetic Ministry*, Frank Damazio writes:

> Jeremiah wore a yoke around his neck through the streets to depict the impending Babylonian bondage (Jeremiah 27–28)....
>
> Isaiah walked naked and barefoot for three years, symbolizing that Egypt and Ethiopia were at the hands of Assyria (Isaiah 20:1–6)....
>
> Ezekiel was commanded to lie upon his left side for 390 days and upon his right side for 40 days. The number of days represented the number of years that Israel had disobeyed and forsaken God throughout their history (Ezekiel 4:4–8)....
>
> Ezekiel was commanded to shave his hair and beard and scatter some of the hair, symbolizing the scattering of a portion of the Jews to various parts of the earth (Ezekiel 5:1–4)....
>
> Ahijah, upon meeting [King] Jeroboam, rent his garment in twelve pieces, symbolizing the division of his kingdom (1 Kings 11:30–31).[23]

And in the New Testament, we see Agabus binding himself with the apostle Paul's belt, "symbolizing what the Jews were going to do to [Paul] in Jerusalem (Acts 21:10–14)."[24]

Damazio also writes about how God instructed certain prophets to name their children using prophetically symbolic concepts:[25]

---

23. Frank Damazio, *Developing the Prophetic Ministry* (Portland, OR: City Christian Publishing, 1983), 19–20. I want to acknowledge Damazio's thorough study of this topic, from which I have really benefited.
24. Demazio, *Developing the Prophetic Ministry*, 21.
25. Demazio, 20.

- Isaiah's children included Shear-jashub, meaning "a remnant shall return,"[26] and Maher-shalal-hash-baz, which means "swift is the plunder, speedy is the prey."[27]

- Hosea's children included Jezreel, which literally means "visit the bloodshed of Jezreel on the house of Jehu,"[28] Lo-ruhamah, which means "not having obtained mercy,"[29] and Lo-ammi, which means "not my people."[30] This latter name was as if Hosea were saying, "That isn't my child." Yeah, it would be intense to grow up hearing your dad say, "You ain't my baby."

God can be demonstrative! The following are a few other biblical examples of His being dramatic with prophetic actions:

- When the law was given, clouds came, lightning flashed, and Mount Sinai trembled. (See Exodus 19:16–18.)

- When Jesus was crucified and resurrected, darkness fell on the land, the earth shook, the veil of the temple was torn in two, and the graves of many saints opened; these saints were raised to life and walked into Jerusalem. Whoa! (See Matthew 27:45–53.)

- On the first day of Pentecost after the resurrection, the people experienced supernatural wind, fire, noise, energy, and "inebriation." (See Acts 2:1–21.)

When God wants to make a point, He will! Should we label that as excessive? What is excessive? We measure this issue by our own experiences. What is currently "normal" for us may not be normal to God. I want God to come and demonstrate His love and His power in His way. Our role is to stand strong in the anointing, confident that God knows what He's doing.

---

26. See Isaiah 7:3 NASB, NASB95, ESV, note a.
27. See Isaiah 8:1 NASB, note b.
28. See Hosea 1:4 NASB, NASB95, note a.
29. See Hosea 1:6 NASB, note b.
30. See Hosea 1:9 NASB, NASB95, note b.

INTERPRETING AND JUDGING PROPHETIC GESTURES AND ACTIONS

When we seek to interpret these prophetic gestures and actions so that we know what to do with them, we need to remember that they may be the spontaneous movement of the Holy Spirit upon a person, or they may also be premeditative gestures and actions demonstrating a message, a prayer, or worship. I do not advocate accepting all gestural communications as being prophetic and biblical. But we also should not dismiss these communications just because we do not understand them. Always search the Scriptures, test the spirits (see 1 John 4:1), and, when possible, interview the person who demonstrated the gesture to hear about what happened from their point of view.

My friend Stacy Campbell has been a forerunner in an ecstatic form of prophecy. When she prophesies, her head will often move rapidly from side to side, as if she is shaking her head. I don't know how she can do that and not get vertigo! We can have bodily reactions to Holy Spirit empowerment. We will react physically and emotionally to the glory of God drawing near. Let's stand in the place of wisdom and grace to hear what God is saying and to see what God is doing.

Here are a few good questions to ask as you seek to interpret and also judge the expression of supernatural gestural communications:

- "What are you praying for and seeking?" Are the people asking for more of God Himself, not just for more manifestations? Then they will get more of God. Our goal is to receive God Himself.

- "Are you seeking and asking for God? Is Jesus your central focus?" Are they humble and exalting Jesus? Then the Holy Spirit will come in answer to their prayers!

- "Are you asking for the gift of discernment?" This is a gift that we need to ask for and cultivate to ensure that the activity is of the Holy Spirit and not merely fleshly zeal or a sincere person trying to help God out. We must also be open to the issue that there may be a mixture of light and darkness at work and/or that the activity is demonically inspired.

- "Is the atmosphere peaceful (even amid what can feel chaotic)?" If the answer is yes, then these manifestations could be signs of the Holy Spirit's presence. Jesus is the Prince of Peace.

- "Is the fruit ultimately good?" Other fruit demonstrated in people's lives could be an increased devotional life, service and faithfulness in marriage, and a growing desire to be in worship before the Lord—all resulting in the fruit of the Spirit. If the outcome is fruitfulness and service before Christ, then the manifestation or activity is being initiated by God. (See Galatians 5:22–25; 2 Peter 1:5–8.)

If God, in His sovereignty, chooses during seasons of divine visitation to do His work with or without phenomena, that is His choice. Additionally, it is of no benefit to have manifestations but have no lasting fruit. Ultimately, what God is after is a willing, humble heart. We must stand strong over time knowing that what we sow, we will reap. We may stumble through the many ways God wants to communicate to us and through us, so let's be patient with each other as we learn and grow in the Spirit.

PRAYER TO GROW IN UNDERSTANDING PROPHETIC ACTIONS

Gracious Father, in the mighty name of Jesus, I want to learn to receive and discern these prophetic ways of the Holy Spirit's distinct communications language. I long to grow in my understanding of these supernatural encounters, their purpose, and their proper place in my life. Help me to increase in my discernment of Your ways so that I can grow into maturity in Christ Jesus. I declare that I need more of Your gifts, presence, and power! Move in, upon, and through me with greater effectiveness and impact. I want to bring forth the fruit of Your kingdom, and I do not want to major on minors. Keep me from traps, ditches, and excessiveness as I welcome genuine supernatural encounters with and through the Holy Spirit. For the glory of God, amen and amen!

8

KEYS TO UNLOCKING SUPERNATURAL ENCOUNTERS

"I will give you the keys of the kingdom of heaven;
whatever you bind on earth will be bound in heaven, and whatever
you loose on earth will be loosed in heaven."
—Matthew 16:19 (NIV)

After I moved from Kansas City to the greater Nashville area, I became fascinated by doors and gates, most likely because of my travels to the United Kingdom, other European countries, and the Middle East. So, I leaned in and started to learn about gates and doors. After a year of research, I came to some profound theological conclusions, which I'll share with you in this chapter.

Jesus promised to give us keys—plural—to the kingdom of heaven, and you're going to discover some biblical keys you may have not considered that will unlock supernatural encounters for yourself and others. Today, keys come in many shapes and sizes. What I want you to remember as we move forward together is that little keys can open big doors—sometimes huge doors, even gates.

KEYS TO OPEN BIG DOORS: POWER, AUTHORITY, AND BOLDNESS

In the revelation that he received, the apostle John heard Jesus say, *"I am He who lives, and was dead, and behold, I am alive forevermore. Amen. And I have the keys of Hades and of Death"* (Revelation 1:18). The keys of God's kingdom have also been transferred to Christ-followers for the task of making disciples. (See Matthew 16:19; 28:19.) And, as believers in Christ Jesus, we are called to be enforcers of His kingdom realm. Romans 16:20 declares, *"The God of peace will soon crush Satan under your feet"* (Romans 16:20 NLT).

What are the keys of God's kingdom? There are many! Luke 9:1 reveals two significant keys: *"Then He called His twelve disciples together and gave them power and authority over all demons, and to cure diseases."* Luke 10:19, recording the words of Jesus, reveals these same two keys of power and authority: *"Behold, I give you the authority to trample on serpents and scorpions, and over all the power of the enemy."*

Another key is found in Hebrews 4:16, which says, *"Let us therefore come boldly to the throne of grace, that we may obtain mercy and find grace to help in time of need."* What are the keys? Not only the power and authority that God gives us, but also the confidence to *"come boldly to the throne of grace."* We do not have to approach God crawling on our knees. If you are in a time of need, don't come begging—come boldly! *"For God has not given us a spirit of fear, but of power and of love and of a sound mind"* (2 Timothy 1:7).

Recently, I had a dream in which I was given a message. In this dream, I felt like I was Isaiah the prophet opening an Old Testament-like scroll. As I unfurled the scroll, a script opened before my eyes, and words reflecting 2 Timothy 1:7 appeared: "I have not given you the spirit of fear." I understood in my knower that the "fear" being referred to was not just about being timid. This was a message to me about cowardice and boldness. The Greek word translated as "*fear*" in this verse is not typical. I didn't know this until I had the dream. This verse could be rendered, "For God has not given us the spirit of cowardice." A kingdom key for unlocking the anointing is that we are to come to God boldly because, in Jesus, we are not cowards.

I am just getting hold of this revelation right now for a fresh wave of grace for my own life, and I feel an authority to speak this to you: You have not received a spirit of cowardice but of power, love, and a sound mind. Amen and amen!

Keys are personal tools, and you must learn to use the keys for yourself. God gives each of us personal responsibility to care for the keys He entrusts to us. We can, in cowardice, be weak and become overly reliant on other people, expecting them to do for us what God wants us to do. Yet taking personal responsibility means accepting the call of God to rise up by grace for Jesus's sake, for your sake, and for others' sake.

Jesus issued a warning in Luke 11:52 in which He rebuked the lawyers, or the experts in the Mosaic law,[31] because they had the key of knowledge but wouldn't use it. He told them, "*For you have taken away the key of knowledge. You did not enter in yourselves, and those who were entering in you hindered.*" Jesus wanted them to use their learning to open the door so others could come in too. If we are to help people do this, we must keep the focus personal and remain flexible.

MAKE IT PERSONAL AND STAY FLEXIBLE

The true supernatural is always personal, and the most effective, lasting ministry is deeply personal. As we flow in the anointing, we need

---

31. Luke 11:52 NASB, note a.

to ensure that we help others take what they are experiencing and focus it on Jesus and a personal relationship with Him.

God notices who is reaching out to Him. I love this about Jesus. Luke 8:45 records Jesus asking, *"Who touched Me?"* as He was being bounced around by a throng of people. Jesus felt one contact with someone more deeply than all the others when a woman reached through the crowd to touch His clothing so she could be healed. This woman not only touched the hem of Jesus's garment, but she also touched His heart. *"Who touched Me?"* He asked. As we walk in the anointing, not only do we impact people, but we also touch the heart of God by moving in a sensitive, personal manner. I have always wanted to touch people's lives, and I have always wanted to touch God. But now I realize that I touch the heart of God when I touch people personally. Yes, the true supernatural is always personal.

The supernatural also requires flexibility. Jesus said, *"The wind blows where it wishes, and you hear the sound of it, but you do not know where it is coming from and where it is going; so is everyone who has been born of the Spirit"* (John 3:8 NASB). You can feel the wind; you can hear the wind. You cannot see the wind, but you can see its effects. You do not know where it comes from, and you do not know where it is headed. Instruments like a sail on a sailboat can harness the wind into effective power. But you have to know how to do it.

Maneuvering a sailboat requires flexibility to produce consistent forward motion, and "tacking" is an essential skill in this regard. Unlike a motorboat, a sailboat cannot move directly against the wind. Because of this, sailors reposition their sails to change the direction of the front of their boat from going into the wind to moving across the wind. By doing so, they can sail in an upwind direction.

Similarly, standing strong in the anointing and in the supernatural activity that results from it requires flexibility. You may position your sail and start to make headway, but then the wind shifts, and if you don't reposition yourself, you'll end up in the wrong place. At times, it may even seem as though you're pointed away from where you want to go. That's how the anointing works sometimes. To use another analogy, you get a curveball, but that's the pitch God wants you to hit. The good news is that you're not alone. There are others taking their turn standing at the plate, anticipating what might be coming, postured to be flexible so they can hit whatever comes their way. This is what it means to be born of the Spirit.

Let's now consider the proper use of the keys that God gives as we look at some specific keys to the supernatural from the life of Elisha the prophet.

NINE KEY LESSONS FROM THE LIFE OF ELISHA

We need the anointing in order to break yokes of slavery—literally and figuratively—and to discern God-sized solutions for those in crisis and need of rescue. A biblical account of debt slavery may be found in the book of 2 Kings. From this story, I want to suggest prophetically nine keys for standing strong in the anointing and unlocking supernatural encounters. Read the full account with me from 2 Kings 4:1–7:

> *A certain woman of the wives of the sons of the prophets cried out to Elisha, saying, "Your servant my husband is dead, and you know that your servant feared the* Lord. *And the creditor is coming to take my two sons to be his slaves." So Elisha said to her, "What shall I do for you? Tell me, what do you have in the house?" And she said, "Your maidservant has nothing in the house but a jar of oil." Then he said, "Go, borrow vessels from everywhere, from all your neighbors—empty vessels; do not gather just a few. And when you have come in, you shall shut the door behind you and your sons; then pour it into all those vessels, and set aside the full ones." So she went from him and shut the door behind her and her sons, who brought the*

vessels to her; and she poured it out. Now it came to pass, when the vessels were full, that she said to her son, "Bring me another vessel." And he said to her, "There is not another vessel." So the oil ceased. Then she came and told the man of God. And he said, "Go, sell the oil and pay your debt; and you and your sons live on the rest."

What are the strategic keys from this passage?

1. *Invest in the next generation.* The enemy always goes after the younger generation. God wants us to use the anointing on their behalf. Are you willing to take what you have and pour it into the next generation?

2. *Bring what you have.* Too many people are waiting for the next big download from God or another confirmation to step out in faith. Yes, we need revelation and direction from the Holy Spirit. But Elisha asked, *"What do you have…?"*

3. *Find empty vessels, many of them.* Don't find people who are full of themselves and are know-it-alls. Look for those who know they are in need of a physician. (See Matthew 9:12.) Jesus wants His house filled. (See Luke 14:15–23.) Find those who are hungry and thirsty.

4. *Shut the door.* If you don't learn to have a personal life, you won't have a life. This includes a personal life with Jesus and with those to whom He wants you to minister. Jesus said, *"Your Father who sees in secret will reward you openly"* (Matthew 6:6). Not everything should be public. Some of our most important work is meant to be done in private.

5. *Pour out the oil.* After you find the empty vessels and shut the door, pour out the anointing you have into them. Some things are caught, and others are taught, and this is God's design for

multiplication in His kingdom. We pour out what we have, and He gives us more.

6. *Set apart the full vessels.* Fill other people up and then send them out. Acts 13:2 (NIV, ESV) records a time when the Holy Spirit spoke and said, *"Set apart for me Barnabas and Saul for the work to which I have called them."* In the same way, there will be a point when those whom you have been pouring into will be full, and it will be time to set them apart unto the Lord for His service.

7. *Obey.* How silly might the woman's sons have felt as they were running around the village gathering containers from the neighbors? How did they respond when they were asked, "What are you going to do with all those jars?" I can hear their excuse: "Oh, my mom's working on something. I don't know what's going on. But thanks for the jar!" And then, what must it have been like for the woman to be surrounded by all those vessels as she held just one flask of oil in her hand and perhaps wondered, "What in the world am I doing?" Wow, but look at what happened! Obey God, even if it's something little that you feel like the Holy Spirit has told you to do.

8. *Recognize that the flow stops when the need is met.* Sometimes the anointing stops flowing because there is a hindrance; perhaps pride has entered in, seeking the Lord has waned, or a demonic entity has found entrance, and discernment is needed to remove the obstacle in Jesus's name. Ask God questions to discern the issue. Other times, the oil of the anointing is no longer flowing because your task is completed! You haven't done anything wrong; you have done something right!

9. *Don't keep the anointing only in the house.* Elisha told the woman to go and sell the oil so that she and her sons could live. God has a wonderful plan for your life and for your family, and He wants you to prosper. That means you can't just keep the anointing in

the house. Get out of the house, adopt a new mindset, use the anointing, and see all that God wants to do.

CLEARING OUT HINDRANCES BLOCKING THE WAY

In each of our lives, there can be hindrances blocking the way toward a clear flow of the supernatural. To experience the blessings God has for us, we must call on the searchlight of the Holy Spirit to bring conviction, fresh insight, and cleansing into those very areas where there have been strongholds from the past. Blockages can be identified and removed through the name and the blood of the Lord Jesus Christ!

I've just been going through another one of those seasons when I felt the Holy Spirit say to me personally, "I'm coming to cleanse My house." For years, I have prayed many kinds of cleansing prayers, and there are certain seasons when I am more intentional about praying these prayers, asking the Holy Spirit to identify hindrances. So, I set out to pray again through some issues in my life—disappointments and hurts—to cleanse my "house." Shortly afterward, I had a dream about going through a home inspection.

I want you to know that God cares about whatever it is that you care about. When I woke up from this supernatural dream, I knew that I had to get a physical home inspection for mold. I originally had thought "I'm going to cleanse My house" was only a spiritual message. I didn't want to carry over excess baggage into the next season. God was coming to cleanse His house. But then I had the dream and woke up with the idea of mold on my mind. I felt prompted to do a search for mold in the natural and, the next day, had a crew come to inspect my home. Within a day, they found three forms of white mold all incorporated or infested under my house. For the next three days, I had a professional crew come and cleanse my whole house, inside and out.

Mold had gotten into my house and was a hindrance blocking my health. I had experienced ongoing infections in my sinuses, and I just couldn't get better. After three infections, I finally scheduled an appointment to see an ear, nose, and throat (ENT) specialist. But, in the meantime, I had been praying cleansing prayers and had had these dream encounters.

At my appointment, the ENT specialist took his scope and put it in my ear. I could see a magnified image of my ear on a screen in front of me. The specialist said, "You do a really good job at cleansing your body."

"Huh?" I thought. "There's no infection? What did he say?"

"You do a really good job of cleansing your body." Then, he added, "There's no infection in your house." He actually used the word *house*. Continuing, he said, "There's no sign of an infection. I don't see any mold. There's no need for a CT scan, and I don't believe that there's any need for nasal surgery. I going to take a deep, deep, mold culture. We'll see. I'll let you know." He finished with, "Drink more water. I'll see you in a month."

What an amazing occurrence of supernatural events. Isn't it remarkable how God speaks to us and cares for us? The Holy Spirit told me He was coming to cleanse my house and that it was time for an inspection. And that's exactly what He did.

I'm here to tell you that there are keys to supernatural encounters, and God is coming to identify hindrances that are blocking the way to them. Some of those hindrances will be spiritual, but God will even deal with things in the natural. God will help to remove the hindrances so we can receive His blessings. Amen!

IDENTIFYING AND REPLACING UNGODLY BELIEFS

While we need to be cleansed from spiritual hindrances, there are additional blockages we must identify and remove, such as ungodly beliefs. According to 2 Corinthians 10:5, we are to be *"casting down arguments and every high thing that exalts itself against the knowledge of God, bringing every thought into captivity to the obedience of Christ."* Ungodly beliefs can also be called strongholds of the mind.

We are to replace these ungodly belief structures with godly beliefs. First Corinthians 2:16 tells us that *"we have the mind of Christ."* For example, if the ungodly belief is, "Nothing ever goes right in my life," it can be replaced with, "Something good is just about to happen," or the truth from Romans 8:28 that *"all things work together for good to those who love God, to those who are the called according to His purpose."* We replace those ungodly belief structures with scriptural, godly beliefs.

I speak to myself regularly from Joel 3:10 (NASB95): *"Let the weak say, 'I am a mighty man.'"* Recent health issues have made me feel progressively weaker. I could feel myself fading. But instead of identifying with such weakness, we can put on the mind of Christ. When we are weak, we know the truth from God's Word that says, *"My grace is sufficient for you, for my power is made perfect in weakness"* (2 Corinthians 12:9 NIV, ESV).

The Levitical priests, who were descendants of Zadok the priest, as recorded in Ezekiel 44, were set apart to minister unto the Lord. They were given strict orders concerning with what and how they were to clothe themselves. They could not wear any wool clothing. (See verse 17.) This was a prophetic symbol that, in the presence of the Lord, no sweat was allowed. One blockage to the anointing is strife, but a key to unlocking the higher realms of supernatural encounters with God is the lost art of resting in faith. Thou shalt not sweat it!

IT'S ALL BY GRACE

Grace. What a beautiful word, and what an amazing gift from God. Grace is the supernatural enablement of God to be all that He has called you to be and to do all that He has called you to do. Ephesians 2:10 in *The Passion Translation* gives a glorious picture of what God's grace has provided: *"We have become his poetry, a re-created people that will fulfill the destiny he has given each of us, for we are joined to Jesus, the Anointed One. Even before we were born, God planned in advance our destiny and the good works we would do to fulfill it!"*

The riches we experience are at Christ's expense. Because of grace, His mercy is granted to the undeserving and the ill-deserving. Anything and everything we have is because of God's grace. We have no reason to boast. You might think that this humble state would cause a person to be insecure and lack confidence. Quite the contrary. God's grace empowers and encourages confidence because we know we have God's favor and that the outcome of our life is in His very capable hands.

It's not surprising, then, that most of the epistles in the New Testament begin with, *"Grace to you and peace,"* or a similar salutation, and most of them end with something like, "The grace of the Lord Jesus Christ be with you." The grace of God makes us attractive. If we don't have the grace of God, we may have the truth, but no one will be attracted to it. A legalistic "gospel" is unattractive, and legalism can be present in every part of the body of Christ. Just because you don't follow a liturgy but try to flow with the Holy Spirit doesn't mean you're not a legalist in certain areas. We need God's grace in order to flow in the anointing of the Spirit and to bear the fruit of the Spirit.

How do we receive the grace that unlocks supernatural encounters? It isn't by trying harder! The answer is very clear: humble yourself. James 4:6–7, 1 Peter 5:5–6, and Proverbs 3:34 convey the same idea: be humble. Why? Because *"God opposes the proud but gives grace to the humble"* (James 4:6 ESV, NLT). So, stop striving. You can't earn supernatural encounters. They come by grace. Hebrews 6:1 classifies *"repentance from dead works and…faith toward God"* as basic foundational principles.

Dead works are what we do by our own efforts to try to obtain righteousness and God's favor.

One of the primary traps Satan sets after he has lost a person to the kingdom of God is to get that person *working* for Jesus instead of *trusting* in Jesus. Paul called out the Galatians for doing this. He even referred to this mindset as *"an evil spell"* (Galatians 3:1 NLT). Then, he said, *"How foolish can you be? After starting your new lives in the Spirit, why are you now trying to become perfect by your own human effort?"* (verse 3 NLT). It is the blood of Jesus that saves us from dead works so we can serve the living God. (See Hebrews 9:14.) If we are in Christ, we are His righteousness, and we have His favor. As we take care of the inward work of the heart, the Holy Spirit takes care of the external works of our hands and makes them acceptable to the Master. All grace is in Jesus! The more of Jesus that is in us, the more grace we will have for every situation. (See John 1:12, 16–17.)

I started this chapter by saying that little keys can open big doors. I have shared a number of "little" keys, but maybe they're not so little: power, authority, boldness, flexibility, obedience, humility, perseverance to overcome hindrances and to develop a biblical mindset, and God's grace. Whoa! These are big keys in the kingdom of God that can help you to avoid the traps and receive the blessings of walking in the anointing of the Holy Spirit.

Supernatural encounters are gifts—jewels of grace. These jewels are the manifested presence of the Holy Spirit—visible expressions of our adornment as the bride of Christ. Grace beautifies the bride, and part of our growth in the supernatural realm comes from believing that the Holy Spirit wants to adorn us, as Christ's bride, with ever-increasing grace gifts of revelation! Express your heart to God—right now—telling Him that you want to be a candidate, that you *are* a candidate, to receive keys to unlocking the supernatural by grace.

PRAYER TO UNLOCK NEW REALMS OF SUPERNATURAL ENCOUNTERS

Heavenly Father, in the great name of Jesus my Lord, I choose to be a faithful steward of the keys of Your kingdom. I make a commitment to use the keys of knowledge for myself and for the sake of others. Turn on the searchlight of the Holy Spirit, reveal any hindrances that are in my way, and remove them by the blood of Jesus. I declare that I am receiving new keys of revelation and fresh purity in my heart, all by grace. I am being propelled into new dimensions of supernatural encounters by faith, and I eagerly anticipate new adventures with the Holy Spirit. I am grateful for the times in which I live! All for the glory of God. Amen and amen!

9

YOUR INVITATION TO GOD ENCOUNTERS

"After these things I looked, and behold, a door standing open in heaven. And the first voice which I heard was like a trumpet speaking with me, saying, 'Come up here, and I will show you things which must take place after this.'"
—Revelation 4:1

There are many people who are highly talented, but since they don't offer back to God what He gave to them, they're left to the limitation of their talents, even though those talents are quite amazing. Then there are those who appear to have limited talents but who give them to God, and He puts "super" in front of their "natural" so that they become supernaturally natural and naturally supernatural. That is why I say that God is an equal-opportunity employer. He invites anyone to come to Him for His "super" to add to their "natural."

Let me tell you a story about a very famous person who did not start out famous at all. You may have heard of healing evangelist Kathryn Kuhlman. But did you know that she grew up in a little country town called Concordia, Missouri, not far from where I grew up in Warrensburg, Missouri? I had the honor of watching her final television broadcast. My seeing it was a divine accident, or you could say it was a divine appointment. I will never forget watching this peculiar, red-headed woman on television.

I distinctly remember Kathryn Kuhlman saying that she was not God's first choice or second choice for her supernatural ministry. She said that she was not even God's third choice because, as she wrote in her book *A Glimpse into Glory*,

> The job I am doing is a man's job. I work hard.... I can outwork five men put together....
>
> ...But no man was as willing to pay the price. I was just naive enough to say "Take nothing, and use it." And He has been doing that ever since.[32]

I recall her saying on that broadcast, "But I said yes. And God chose someone"—these were her words—"who was ugly, who was tall, who was a redhead and didn't have much to offer. But what I offered was availability."

I heard those words and thought, "But you're world-famous. There have been few in contemporary church history who have moved in miracles like Kathryn Kuhlman did." She wasn't Pentecostal. She wasn't highly educated. And she was naturally somewhat eccentric. So I'm here to tell you that an availability for God encounters is your best ability. God will put "super" behind, and with, your natural. Once more, the best ability is your availability. When the God of the universe comes to

---

32. Kathryn Kuhlman and Jamie Buckingham, *A Glimpse into Glory* (Old Tappan: Logos International, 1979), 30–31.

you, all He is looking for is what we all have to give Him: our yes. Have you given Him your yes? Our journey in the supernatural begins with His invitation and our surrender!

We need a big-picture view of what God is looking for. We do this by "coming up higher." This is what the *"voice"* said to John in his revelation: *"Come up here, and I will show you things which must take place after this"* (Revelation 4:1). The big picture, from God's viewpoint, allows us to see details more clearly and in the proper perspective. In this chapter, we will look from God's perspective and see His invitation to encounter Him and release encounters through the anointing.

GOD'S TIMELINE FOR HIS INVITATION

The story of Esther in the Bible is a prototype for us as believers. In the same way that the king lowered his scepter so Esther could approach the throne and ask for whatever she desired (see Esther 5:1–3), our King's scepter is lowered for us so that we have the right to *"come boldly to the throne of grace, that we may obtain mercy and find grace to help in time of need"* (Hebrews 4:16).

At times, God will say, "What do you *want?*" and not only, "What do you *need?*" The Holy Spirit is saying to every believer who is hungry for more of God, "Come up higher. Come closer. Draw near. I am offering you an invitation into divine participation. I will draw near to you as you draw near to Me. I have a seat at My table waiting just for you. No one can take your place. Come here, My beloved. Draw near!"

With such an awe-inspiring invitation to partner with our Creator, a good question to ask is, "What is the invitation for?" If you received a general invitation to a party, you might wonder what the occasion was for that invitation. God's invitation is for you to participate in the restoration of all things! The events to come will require you to stand strong in the anointing.

Acts 3:19–21 (NIV) gives us a glimpse into that future:

Repent, then, and turn to God, so that your sins may be wiped out, that times of refreshing may come from the Lord, and that he may send the Messiah, who has been appointed for you—even Jesus. Heaven must receive him until the time comes for God to restore everything, as he promised long ago through his holy prophets.

The *New Living Translation* makes the meaning of verse 21 even clearer by saying, "*He must remain in heaven until the time for the final restoration of all things, as God promised long ago through his holy prophets.*" In other words, there is a restraining order on the second coming of Jesus until certain things occur. Hmm. We have been invited to participate in these *"times of refreshing"* before Jesus returns.

Jesus will be retained in heaven until the restoration of all things, spoken about by the holy prophets of old. This includes the full restoration of all five ascension gifts of the Holy Spirit to the body of Christ to their original condition of impact as salt and light. (See Matthew 5:13–14.) Ephesians 4:11–13 (NASB) tells us what that looks like:

He gave some as apostles, some as prophets, some as evangelists, some as pastors and teachers, for the equipping of the saints for the work of ministry, for the building up of the body of Christ; until we all attain to the unity of the faith, and of the knowledge of the Son of God, to a mature man, to the measure of the stature which belongs to the fullness of Christ.

Notice that this verse doesn't say that everyone is an apostle. There's a fad right now where various would-be leaders have name cards, similar to business cards, on which they include their title. So many of these individuals are claiming the title of apostle. A decade ago, everybody wanted to be a prophet. The truth is that God has given different people different gifts for the purpose of empowering every believer to do the works of the Lord Jesus Christ.

Here's a synopsis of what Ephesians 4 tells us: These essential gifts are given for the equipping of every single believer. For what purpose? To build up the body of Christ. For how long? Until we attain the unity of the faith. Has that happened yet? No. Therefore, Jesus is still retained in heaven until this occurs. In the meantime, we pursue coming into the full knowledge of the Son of God, until we become mature followers of Jesus and grow into the fullness of Christ. Wow.

Now, how and when is that going to happen? It is only recently, in contemporary Christianity, that we have begun to recognize that apostles, prophets, evangelists, pastors, and teachers are again being released and empowered to do these works. That is why I and others are making a bold statement that we have entered into the beginning of the second apostolic age of the church.

My dad was a carpenter, and he built furniture. I grew up around that woodworking culture, and I also refurbished old furniture. When you refurbish furniture, you have to work through layers of paint, varnish, and veneers to get back to the original wood. That's the way restoration works. In the same way, the church must go through a process in order to be restored to what the original, first apostolic age of the church looked like. This sounds exciting, but it is a long, tedious, messy process.

The restoration *message* is the gospel of the kingdom. Jesus did not send His disciples out to share the gospel of the church but the gospel of the kingdom. The restoration *method* is preaching this message with purity and power. And the restoration *messengers* are the members of the body of Christ using all of the fivefold ministry gifts of the Spirit.

In the Scriptures, God reveals Himself as being the God of three generations in one: the God of Abraham, Isaac, and Jacob. We need the wisdom of those believers who are older, the resources of those who are middle-aged, and the zeal of those who are younger. Too often, we have the zeal of the younger ones, who often just go out without being covered and joined with others, or the older folks, who sit on a massive amount of experience without being joined to the younger generations. Those in the middle generation often squander their resources or keep those resources to themselves. We need all three aspects—wisdom, resources, and zeal—to have the fullness of supernatural encounters. This convergence is a new wineskin that is able to hold the new wine. God wants to take the best of the past moves of the Spirit and blend them together to create the convergence of the ages. He does serve, like Jesus did, the best wine at the last.[33]

HOPE SOLUTIONISTS[34]

In these last days, I believe God is giving a specific call to any who will listen. That invitation is to be a "hope solutionist" with divine intelligence. When the world has no more solutions, when darkness covers the earth, that is the appointed time for God's light-bearers to arise and shine. (See Isaiah 60:1–3.) When human beings have no more answers, the supernatural anointing will rest upon men and women alike who carry God-remedies. These are the hope solutionists who have a positive expectation of good—disciples of the Lord Jesus Christ who have been forged in the fire of God and who come forth declaring, "Something good is just about to happen!"[35]

For the last eighteen-plus years, I have experienced a great deal of suffering and trauma: a nine-year battle against cancer; losing my wife; enduring a failed back surgery, resulting in chronic pain; and so much

---

33. See my book *The Lifestyle of a Prophet*, particularly the reading for Day 21, "Paradigm Shifts for a Prophetic Lifestyle," for more details on this subject.
34. See my twenty-minute presentation on being a hope solutionist entitled "Creativity and Divine Intelligence," June 13, 2021, uploaded by King Jesus Miami YouTube channel, https://www.youtube.com/watch?v=RdCGp0YLWZg.
35. See my book *Tell Your Heart to Sing Again* (Savage, MN: Broadstreet Publishing, 2020) to glean real-life answers on this subject.

more. All of this has felt like a downward spiral. I have been forced to learn important lessons, and I have firsthand experience that *"God causes all things to work together for good to those who love God, to those who are called according to His purpose"* (Romans 8:28 NASB). God didn't cause all these things to happen to me, but, as I brought them to Him, He took my mess and made something good come from it. I believe I'm more like Christ today than I was eighteen years ago, and, through God's grace, I've seen good fruit come from my life and ministry.

What has the last eighteen years brought you? Can you believe God is causing all things to work together for good for you? I want to invite you on the journey with me into hope. You could be the next hope solutionist. I'm calling forth hope ambassadors who bring supernatural solutions for such a time as this. (See Esther 4:14.)

Hope solutionists carry the anointing of the *"seven Spirits of God"* (Revelation 3:1; 4:5), or the *"sevenfold Spirit of God"* (Revelation 3:1; 4:5 NLT), into the seven cultural spheres of society. Isaiah 11:1–3 (NASB) lists these seven aspects of God that Isaiah prophesied would characterize the Messiah:

> *Then a shoot will spring from the stem of Jesse, and a Branch from his roots will bear fruit. The Spirit of the* Lord *will rest on Him, the spirit of wisdom and understanding, the spirit of counsel and strength, the spirit of knowledge and the fear of the* Lord. *And He will delight in the fear of the* Lord, *and He will not judge by what His eyes see, nor make decisions by what His ears hear.*

The following list confirms what we see in other places in Scripture: multifaceted expressions of the Holy Spirit manifested in the life of Jesus that are for us today. God invites you to be a hope solutionist who will embody these supernatural expressions of Jesus:[36]

---

36. See my book *God Encounters Today* and its corresponding materials for more on this topic.

- Spirit of the Lord
- Spirit of wisdom
- Spirit of understanding
- Spirit of counsel
- Spirit of strength
- Spirit of knowledge
- Spirit of the fear of the Lord

God wants the fullness of the Spirit to rest upon His people in every area of kingdom life and in every sphere of culture. There are supernatural encounters available in the heart of God for each person and for every realm, including the realms of family, government, education, economy, the church, arts and entertainment, media, and more.[37] When Jesus commissioned His disciples to go into all the world, He meant *all* the world! Where has God placed you right now, and where might He be leading you to bring the character and power of Christ? You are to be supernaturally natural and naturally supernatural.[38]

Here is the key: In the past, we relegated supernatural encounters only—oh, this is so wrong—to the church. Huh? Yeah. That is why, in part, we have not had the impact that we're supposed to have as salt and light in the world. In our attempt not to be "of the world" (see Jesus's words in John 15:18–19), we've removed ourselves from being *in* the world. This must change! We are salt and light—this is our nature as followers of Christ—and we are to carry supernatural encounters into every realm of society. I'll say it again: God wants the fullness of the

---

37. See my book *The Prophet* (Shippensburg, PA: Destiny Image, 2019)—specifically chapter 9, "Influencing the Seven Spheres of Society"—for more on this subject.
38. See my book *Living a Supernatural Life* (Bloomington, MN: Chosen Books, 2013) for more on this subject.

Spirit to rest upon His people in every area of kingdom life, in every area or sphere of culture.

Allow me to make this point more personal. Michal Ann and I did not raise our children to pick up our mantle and carry on our specific ministry. I'm not saying it's wrong for an heir to be the successor of a church or ministry. In other words, so-and-so has a church, and then, after they retire or scale back after thirty years of leading that church, their son or daughter takes over as the lead pastor. That just wasn't our intention. Instead, we sought to build a culture of creativity so they could discover their gifts and be the best they could be.

Our oldest son, Justin, is in the TV and film industry in Los Angeles. Believe me, it's a polluted industry, but he's salt and light there, and he is brilliant at his craft, having won a Peabody Award as a senior editor on a documentary project. While she was growing up, I used to tell our oldest daughter, GraceAnn, that she was going to need a lot of initials behind her name. Well, she earned her master's degree at the Art Institute of Chicago, and, among other things, she practices and teaches art therapy today. Our youngest son, Tyler, loved gaming when he was growing up. Today, he has a degree in game, art, and design, and he works for Armada Content. Lastly, there is our youngest daughter, Rachel, who has training in modeling, acting, and songwriting. She is a successful social entrepreneur, a singer, and a songwriter. All my children are married, have families, and serve Jesus in the secular world.

God has supernatural encounters for every person, no matter their age, role, gender, ethnicity, or profession. If you are a firefighter, pay attention to the word of knowledge that tells you to get out of the house. Or, if you work in retail, you need a lot of strength! Let it be the strength of the Spirit, and lean into the Spirit of knowledge to be the best at what you do. If you manage people (this goes for parents at home too), don't lean on your own understanding. Instead, draw upon the Spirit of wisdom and understanding in the way you deal with others. If you're leading a company, walk in the spirit of the fear of the Lord.

Years ago, when I worked at a hospital and nursing home, I would refer to my chart to pray over my patients every day. If you're in the medical service industry, you do a lot of hard, ugly stuff. You know the kind of work I did, and I imagine that you are doing the same. Serve with all of your heart in the Spirit of Jesus. As you are faithful in the natural, God will put His super with your natural. You are called to be in the world and to be the best you can be in it. You can walk in the supernatural power of the Spirit in a profoundly impactful manner.

DIVINE INTELLIGENCE

Along with being filled with the Holy Spirit, I believe hope solutionists are also called to operate in divine intelligence. Daniel will be our end-time role model for this quality. He is an example for us of how to live a life of excellence in the world system. You may also want to read-pray through the entire book of Daniel.

I remember reading the book of Daniel years ago and thinking that the events described there took place over a period of about ten years of Daniel's life. Similarly, when I read about the virtuous woman in Proverbs 31, I thought, "Wow! She got a lot done in one year!" I didn't understand that the Bible provides us with an expansive overview of this woman's entire lifetime. In the same way, the book of Daniel provides us with a glimpse, an overview, of his whole life. Daniel both started well and ended well.

By the way, if you did not start well, you can turn toward God and all that He has for you at any point in your life. I used to say that "God is the God of a second chance." I threw away that saying a long time ago. Our God is the God of a fifty-millionth chance—either to turn to Him for the first time or to embrace His full call for your life. That is how good our Father is. Let that sink in. God forgives you and uses your past mistakes for your very own good. You need to hear and know that.

Now, I have personally had two distinct windows of time in which I went into a zone where I experienced a supernatural realm that included, but went beyond, the gifts of the Spirit. They appeared to include the seven spirits of God as I stepped into the mind of Christ. I believe this is expressed as divine *"intelligence"* in Daniel 1:17 (NASB95): *"God gave them* [Daniel and his friends] *knowledge and intelligence in every branch of literature and wisdom; Daniel even understood all kinds of visions and dreams."*

Daniel had a number of attributes and made various choices that caused him to be a candidate for divine intelligence. He did the following:

- *Developed excellence in character.* Daniel is like no other person in the Bible besides Jesus. He refused to bow his knee to any other god, even under persecution. He stayed true through the fire of trials. He was imprisoned and then cast into a pit with lions (see Daniel 6), but he stayed pure as a man of character. I'm sure other temptations came his way, just as Joseph experienced, but he did not succumb to them. Daniel even demonstrated emotional stability. After Nebuchadnezzar hastily called for the execution of all the wise men in Babylon because they could not explain his dream, Daniel didn't freak out, try to defend himself, or flee the palace. Daniel 2:14 (NASB, NASB95) says, *"Then Daniel replied with discretion and discernment."* Wow.

- *Promoted a culture of honor.* Daniel didn't push away with an attitude the pagan food and wine offered to him. He talked respectfully to the chief official. (See Daniel 1:8–16.) For decades, Daniel served pagan leaders and led the wise men of Babylon faithfully and with integrity, despite the evil they promoted.

- *Sought God consistently.* Even though he was in captivity, he would kneel in his upstairs room in front of his windows that looked toward Jerusalem three times a day—morning, noon, and evening. He had amazing consistency and devotion to God.

- *Became knowledgeable about every form of literature.* After being trafficked from Israel to Babylon as a teenager and enslaved so he could serve in the king's palace, he studied at the school of the Chaldeans, even though he was a Hebrew. He embodied these words of Paul to Timothy: *"Study to show yourself approved by God, a workman who need not be ashamed, rightly dividing the word of truth"* (2 Timothy 2:15 MEV).

These four things are what Daniel himself did. Diligence can take us a long way, but, after that, we are dependent upon God. So where does the divine intelligence come in? Daniel 1:17 (NASB95) says, *"God gave them knowledge and intelligence in every branch of literature and wisdom."* Yes, Daniel studied in the school of the Chaldeans. But then God went beyond Daniel's studies because it says, *"God gave...."* That isn't something that Daniel studied. To me, this is mind-blowing! Diligence takes us just so far, but then God gives, because our assignments are greater than our diligence. When God gives, He gives only His best!

There are a number of modern-day examples of Daniels who have divine intelligence.[39] One is Dr. Ben Carson. Years ago, for more than six weeks, I was living in a divine bubble of God's tangible presence. The Lord spoke to me about Dr. Carson, saying, "Have you considered Dr. Ben Carson?" At that time, I did not even know who Ben Carson was, but the Holy Spirit started talking to me about this man of brilliant intelligence and how He was raising him up as a role model in the nation to help change society. I called my older son and said, "Have you

---

39. A ninety-minute discussion between Patricia King and me sharing intriguing information and real-life stories on this topic is available at "Divine Intelligence James Goll and Patricia King XPMedia," James W. Goll YouTube channel, https://youtu.be/pjR3SJla3do.

ever heard of some guy named Ben Carson?" He replied, "Are you kidding me? Haven't you read the book *Gifted Hands*?" I hadn't. He continued, "Didn't you watch his speech at the national prayer breakfast with President Obama? It was awesome!" I didn't know what he was talking about, but the Lord knew and told me a lot about this man. Dr. Carson is an example of a forerunner whom God has raised up—a servant of Christ with divine intelligence—to be what? A hope solutionist!

As you read this, I issue you an invitation. The Holy Spirit invites you embrace all His gifts so that every single follower of Jesus can be built up and equipped to minister by the Spirit in every area of society. Jesus will remain in heaven until we complete this task. Let us do our part to come into the full knowledge of the Son of God until we grow into the fullness of Christ and walk in supernatural encounters that proclaim the kingdom of God. When darkness covers the earth, a great light will shine so brightly that even kings will come to the brightness of its shining. (See Isaiah 60:1–3.) In that hour, God will raise up His hope solutionists to carry the brightness of His Word to pierce this present darkness. This is that hour—and we are invited to be those hope solutionists!

PRAYER TO GROW INTO THE FULL STATURE OF CHRIST

God Almighty, I come to You in the gracious name of Jesus Christ. I receive the Holy Spirit's call to "Come up higher" and to receive new blueprints of divine marching orders. I also acknowledge that, according to Ephesians 4:11–12, You have given some to be apostles, prophets, evangelists, pastors, and teachers, to equip the saints to do the work of ministry. Help me to find my place as I join with each generation of believers in a culture of honor. When darkness covers the earth, let Your light come. I want to spread the light and love of Jesus Christ. I desire to walk in hope and be a hope ambassador. In fact, I volunteer to be hope solutionist by the grace of God—to help solve mankind's problems with heaven's answers. Here I am, Lord. Use me! Amen and amen!

# PART THREE

WALKING WISELY IN DIVINE ENCOUNTERS

10

HANDLING COMPLEX SUPERNATURAL EXPERIENCES

"For God has not given us a spirit of fear, but of power and of love and of a sound mind."
—2 Timothy 1:7

Earlier in this book, I shared about having a vivid dream in which I was handed a scroll that said, "I have not given you the spirit of fear." I also explained that a good translation of 2 Timothy 1:7 is "For God has not given us the spirit of cowardice." What I did not previously share is that God sent this message to me at a very strategic time: January 2021. Of course, we know about the chaos of 2020, and the Lord had something to say as we entered 2021. In this dream, Ché Ahn, Cindy Jacobs, and I together released the spirit of boldness upon the body of Christ to confront the spirit of passivity and intimidation that had been permeating the greater society. God wanted to confront the false narrative of political correctness. You may not know that Ché was used to help win a U.S. Supreme Court case that fought for the right of churches to assemble during the pandemic, particularly in California, where Ché lives. That took a great deal of courage, and the Lord was showing me that we needed courage!

And so, I open the last section of this book with a strong, Spirit-inspired reminder: God has not given you the spirit of a coward. This is essential to know in order to stand strong in the anointing, especially when you run into more complex challenges. There are traps to avoid and blessings to embrace, and you will need courage to do both.

I hope I've convinced you that diverse supernatural experiences are possible. They are not only possible, but they are also happening around the world at this moment, facilitated by believers like you who are hungry to move in the anointing of the Spirit. Do you believe this? I pray that you do. Even so, we still need to answer this question: *How do we approach these divine encounters with wisdom—whether they happen to us or to someone else?* That is the subject of this chapter and the focus of the final section of this book.

If you golf, you know that your approach shot determines where your ball will land on the green and, ultimately, how many putts you will need to make to put the ball in the cup. In the same way, let's make a strong approach shot on this subject appropriately so we don't triple bogey! Are you ready for it? The greatest approach…is intimacy with Jesus. So, let's stay close to Him, learn from Him, and then put into practice what He shows us. Okay! Now we're ready to take on some more of these diverse complex supernatural experiences.

OUT-OF-BODY EXPERIENCES

For the topic of out-of-body experiences, our primary Scripture is Ezekiel 8:3, which says, *"The Spirit lifted me up between earth and heaven."* When an out-of-body experience occurs, the person's spirit literally leaves their physical body, and they begin to travel in the spiritual dimension by the Spirit of the Lord. Once they are out there, the surrounding environment does not appear the same to them as it does in the natural because now their spiritual eyes, and not their natural eyes, are seeing. In this unusual experience, the Holy Spirit directs our eyes to see what He wants us to see, in exactly the way He wants. The supernatural is not limited in the way the natural is. You can perceive in the supernatural in ways you don't in the natural. For example, there are colors, sights, and sounds in the supernatural realm that cannot be experienced completely in the natural.

What was the process of being caught up in an out-of-body experience like for Ezekiel? We can see it through the language of the Bible:

- *"Then the Spirit lifted me up, and I heard behind me…"* (Ezekiel 3:12).

- *"So the Spirit lifted me up and took me away"* (Ezekiel 3:14).

- *"He stretched out the form of a hand, and took me by a lock of my hair; and the Spirit lifted me up between earth and heaven, and brought me in visions of God…"* (Ezekiel 8:3).

- *"Then the Spirit lifted me up and brought me to the East Gate of the Lord's house"* (Ezekiel 11:1).

- *"The hand of the Lord came upon me and brought me out in the Spirit of the Lord, and set me down in the midst of the valley"* (Ezekiel 37:1).

- *"The Spirit lifted me up and brought me into the inner court; and behold, the glory of the Lord filled the temple"* (Ezekiel 43:5).

Whoa! Can you imagine what this was like? The words of Scripture help us to see what these out-of-body experiences involved. I have personally had multiple such experiences. I want to be clear that these experiences have never been self-induced. When they occur, I am always in prayer and worship. I do pray to experience everything that's in the Bible, and you can too. But I do not "will" myself into something. As I wrote earlier, God does not need our additives. Projecting yourself into an out-of-body experience is beyond an additive. It's not safe or biblical, and it can even come from the forbidden dark side of the occult dimension.

I have been blessed to have had some rather amazing personal experiences. I had one encounter in which it appeared that I was soaring on the back of an eagle up and down the West Coast of the United States. Now, I said "it appeared." As I have mentioned, there is often a fine line in discerning whether an experience is symbolic or literal. The primary point is the fruit and the meaning of the encounter, not the exact categorization of the complex supernatural realm. This I know: that flying realm seemed real to me at the time! The Holy Spirit, in the form of the keen-sighted eagle, was looking for a place to land.

A few years ago, a friend of mine rode the Avatar Flight of Passage, a 3D flying simulator attraction at Disney's Animal Kingdom. Guests take flight on a native mountain Banshee and soar across the landscape of Pandora. I've not been on that ride yet, but my experience was no less exhilarating. We soared and we hovered over regions, like eagles do, searching for an appropriate location to land and build a nest. We were in search of "Eagle's Landing."

While I was hanging on for dear life, the eagle swooped into an auditorium in Pasadena, California, with which I was familiar. It was filled with spiritually hungry people. The eagle hovered and then landed. Many eagles were now gathering in the arena as heroes of the faith shared their testimonies of great lessons they had learned. Electricity filled the atmosphere as these veterans of the faith were delighted to pass on their lessons the next generation of believers.

I stood at the back, and I was captured by the sight of John Wimber, who was the international leader of the Vineyard movement but was now in the great cloud of witnesses. He was at the front of the auditorium, and there was a radiant glow emanating from him. He was preaching and releasing a message about the Fourth Wave of church history, as he had been a historic, apostolic ambassador of the Third Wave from the mid-1980s into the 1990s.

I was fully alert in this out-of-body experience—in this extraordinary rapt encounter—as John Wimber shared examples from the First, Second, and Third Wave Movements. With the clarity of a statesman, he went on to declare that the Fourth Wave was going to be a convergence of the ages, bringing together the best elements from the previous three waves and carrying a new, distinct mark of transformation. Ambassador Wimber then forcefully announced, "The Fourth Wave has begun!" The shock waves of the Holy Spirit reverberated throughout the room as this declaration was released.

A clear message I received from this encounter was that the supernatural power of the Holy Spirit's gifts will not be able to be contained within the four walls of the church but rather will explode into every sphere of life.[40] It stood out to me that the prophetic eagle of God is searching for places where he can have a resting place to train the next generation and take them beyond renewal and into transformation.

I do not experience this dimension of out-of-body encounters on a regular basis, but they are a part of my prophetic equipment. Recently, when I was in quiet, Christian meditative prayer and worship, I was privileged to have a heavenly encounter that was quite personal and healing. I was taken up higher and higher by the Holy Spirit on a journey until I reached heaven and walked its corridors. I saw some people who had stood against me, and some others who had actually persecuted me in a

---

40. For more about all four waves in church history and this experience, see James Goll, "The Start of the Fourth Wave," September 29, 2012, https://godencounters.com/start-fourth-wave/.

movement that I was once a part of. I was walking down a long corridor toward an auditorium where persevering believers would be honored to tell their major life lessons of overcoming for others to hear. It appeared that I was being prepared to enter this great Hall of Testimony.

As a faceless guide was escorting me down the hallway, I walked by a well-known leader from the Midwest who had recently passed to glory. He stretched out his hand and stopped me. Then he said to me, "I'm so glad that you continued in your journey. I'm so glad that there continue to be pioneers who do not quit and who continue to take new territory for Christ Jesus." It was an amazing healing exchange. While he was alive, I did not have the opportunity to see this leader face-to-face and have personal reconciliation with him, though I had forgiven him and had attempted to seek him out. So, to see him in heaven and to have him touch me and honor me was beyond anything I could ask for or think. Tears come to my eyes as I pen these words. Heavenly encounters are indeed real, and they can be used to bring you messages that your heart yearns to hear. Again, I did not seek this encounter. It came as I was worshipping Jesus.

Let me now offer some words of wisdom and caution:

1. *Counterfeits of all true Holy Spirit-inspired experiences exist.* The difference can be slight and yet very great in purpose and fruit. Once more, we are never to "will" ourselves into such experiences. They are only to be God-initiated. Otherwise, we are participating in self-projection or some rendition of astral projection. When spiritists, sorcerers, New Age practitioners, and witches practice out-of-body experiences without the Holy Spirit and seem to prosper by it, it is because they are already deceived and are not a threat to Satan. Whether they realize it or not, they are already in league with him.

2. *There is a difference between an "actual-appearance" encounter and a "symbolic-representation" encounter.* What does that mean?

We must ask ourselves this question: "Is what I'm experiencing an actual appearance—an apparition—or is it a visual symbol only?" Many people claim to have seen an actual appearance of a saint or the angel Gabriel who came to visit them, when it is only a symbolic visualization of that believer or angel in the great cloud of witnesses from the heavenly realm.

What difference does it make? Well, again, God does not need our help, and humility matters. Do not become overly familiar with the special things of God. When there is an "actual appearance," then a level of authority will come with the encounter. Often, an impartation of some kind occurs. When it is a visually symbolic occurrence alone, it is still quite valid; it can carry the same weight, the same authority, and possibly the same level of commissioning.

So, do not enter a self-induced experience, do not exaggerate your experience, and remember to test the spirits to see if they are from God. Above all, do not let the enemy steal what God has ordained. We do not need to be afraid of these unusual ways of the Holy Spirit, nor do we need to exaggerate them. Watch out for pride that says you were chosen to have an actual visitation by an archangel or by the apostle Paul, when it was perhaps a symbolic manifestation. Stay humble and worship Jesus only!

HEAVENLY VISITATIONS

I wrote in an earlier chapter about the apostle Paul's experience in the third heaven. (See 2 Corinthians 12:2.) The Bible refers to three heavens. The first and lowest heaven is the atmospheric sky that encircles the earth. This is our stellar heaven and might be what we call outer space, where the sun, moon, stars, planets, and galaxies are. (See Genesis 1:14–18.) The mid-heaven, as the Scriptures refer to it, is, of course, the second heaven. Ephesians 6:12 refers to powers and principalities and spirits of wickedness in the heavenly places. The mid-heaven is the abode of Satan and the place where demons and other spiritual powers exist. The third heaven is the highest heaven and the center around which all realms revolve. It is often referred to as paradise. This is the dwelling place of God and His angels, and it is where the justified spirits of the saints reside. (See, for example, Psalm 11:4; Hebrews 12:22–24.)[41]

A heavenly visitation, then, is an out-of-body experience, except that in this case the person's spirit appears to leave the earthly realm, pass through the second or mid-heaven, and go to the highest or third heaven. This can occur while the person is praying, while they are in a trance or have fallen into a deep sleep from the Lord, or when they have a near-death experience or die.

It is believed that Paul heard *"inexpressible words"* and had a truly paradisal experience in the third heaven. He seems to have been immediately caught up into this realm. (See 2 Corinthians 12:2–4.) We cannot tell for certain, but this is possibly the type of experience into which Moses entered. If this was not a circumstance in which he had a heavenly visitation, then he at least experienced an open heaven where he saw the tabernacle and its blueprint in heaven. This occurred when Moses was on Mount Sinai during forty days of consecration and fasting. (See Exodus 24:18; 25:1, 8–9; Hebrews 8:5.)

What will happen when we draw near to God, and He draws near to us? Genesis 5:24 tells us briefly about how Enoch walked with God. Hebrews 11:5 (NLT) explains that Enoch *"was taken up to heaven without dying"* and never returned to earth! The Bible also says about him, *"For before he was taken up, he was known as a person who pleased God"* (verse 5 NLT). Let's also have this as our testimony!

In his book *Falling into Heaven*, my dear friend Mickey Robinson wrote a gripping account of his being in the third heaven. Years ago, while ministering in Cambodia, I prophesied over a man who had also

---

41. My book *The Triumph: Your Comprehensive Guide to Spiritual Warfare* (Minneapolis, MN: Chosen Books, 2024) and its curriculum kit go into detail about the three heavens.

experienced the third heaven. I said to him something like this: "Sir, I see you looking in the mirror and freaking out. It's like you died and went to hell. I see your wife praying over your body. You actually went to hell, didn't you? You came back, and you were raised from the dead. And now you're a prophetic evangelist." As I was saying this, everyone in the crowd who knew him was going crazy because they were familiar with his story.

Here's what had happened to this man: He had died from malaria, and his wife even received his death certificate. People were coming to take his body to the morgue, but his wife persuaded them to wait while she interceded over his dead body. This husband and wife had been Buddhists, but the wife was a recent convert to Christianity. After the man died, his spirit descended into hell. Then he heard his name being called out as his wife was praying over his lifeless body. His spirit ascended and went back into his body. All of a sudden, he knew who Jesus was. He sat up, stood, and went to look in the mirror (just as I had prophesied), and he freaked out. He ran out into the village and went from hut to hut telling everybody about Jesus. It turned out he was now a church planter, and I had seen his supernatural visitation to hell.

Some additional thoughts on this "heavenly" visitation (even though this man went to hell). In the same way that a person can visit the third heaven by having an out-of-body experience, they can also visit the various regions of hell. If they are a sinner, they approach hell by descending—either in death, in a near-death experience, or in a supernatural vision—and they are shown where they are destined to spend eternity unless they accept Jesus Christ as their personal Lord and Savior. Then they are brought back to earth and returned to their body by the mercy of God. If the person is a Christian, the Spirit of the Lord may bring them to hell in such an experience, as well, for the purpose of revealing the suffering torments of the damned. They are then sent back to their body to testify and warn non-Christians to repent and receive Jesus as Lord. That is exactly what happened in the next story.

One time, I was ministering in the state of Minnesota, and I started to declare a word over a particular man. I didn't have a clue who he was. Sometimes I get stuck like an old record and keep repeating a phrase until I feel it goes into the person. I repeated a prophetic phrase over this man twenty-three times in a row, stating that he was going to hell. The prophetic word was recorded, and later I learned in a letter from his wife that they counted how many times I made this statement. Shortly after my prophetic word to him, he visited hell for twenty-three minutes in which he saw the searing flames of hell, felt total isolation, and experienced the putrid and rotting stench, deafening screams of agony, and terrorizing demons there; finally, the strong hand of God lifted him out of the pit. Jesus told him to tell others that He is coming very, very soon. This man's name is Bill Wiese, and he was used to compose a globally famous book entitled *23 Minutes in Hell*.[42]

Multiple times, I have had my own encounters in which I visited heaven, where I have seen my parents and my wife. Let me tell you this: everyone in heaven looks beautiful! But I have not been allowed to remain there. I have been sent back with a message that I must stay here on the earthly side. My assignment on earth is not yet complete. But these visitations have been profound and purposeful. While heaven has an incredible pull on my entire being, I have been seared with this message: "You are here to terrorize the devil!"

STANDING IN THE COUNCIL OF GOD

The last complex supernatural experience I want to share with you is that of standing in the council of God, which overlaps with what the Bible calls the *"great…cloud of witnesses"* (Hebrews 12:1). This can also be an out-of-body experience where a person visits heaven, specifically what the Bible calls the council of God, possibly in a heavenly council

---

42. You can watch Bill's original testimony at "23 Minutes in Hell (Original)—Bill Wiese, 'The Man Who Went To Hell' Author '23 Minutes In Hell,'" Bill Wiese YouTube channel, https://www.youtube.com/watch?v=AYxKRoONrfY. Also see www.23minutesinhell.com.

room, again including an aspect of the great cloud of witnesses. Like other realms of the Spirit, it is accessed either experientially or by faith. This council of the Lord is composed of a group of people in heaven who are meeting in close deliberation, and someone from earth is allowed to listen in or even interact with them. Two illustrations of the council of God in Scripture are the throne room scenes of Daniel 7 and Revelation 3 and 4. The following two additional passages of Scripture will inform our discussion about the council of God, or the great cloud of witnesses:

> *But who has stood in the council of the LORD, that he should see and hear His word? Who has paid attention to His word and listened?… But if they had stood in My council, then they would have announced My words to My people, and would have turned them back from their evil way and from the evil of their deeds.*
> (Jeremiah 23:18, 22 NASB)

> *But you have come to Mount Zion and to the city of the living God, the heavenly Jerusalem, and to myriads of angels, to the general assembly and church of the firstborn who are enrolled in heaven, and to God, the Judge of all, and to the spirits of the righteous made perfect, and to Jesus, the mediator of a new covenant, and to the sprinkled blood, which speaks better than the blood of Abel.*
> (Hebrews 12:22–24 NASB, NASB95)

Why am I referencing the council of God, or the great cloud of witnesses? Because you have the honor to access those who are standing there. Jesus tells us there are many rooms in the Father's house, and I believe there is a council room. He invites some people into the supernatural experience of standing in the council room of heaven to be a part of deliberations with Him. It's an honor that God grants this kind of audience.

"Standing in the council" is a phrase used in some seer-prophetic circles to mean "being there." Sometimes we experience heavenly encounters fully in the body (see, for example, Acts 9:10; 10:3, 19; 18:9), and, at other times, there seems to be an in-between place in which we experience them (see, for example, Acts 10:10; 11:5; 22:17). Full-blown out-of-body encounters are significantly different. (See, for example, Ezekiel 1:1, 3; 3:22; 8:1–11; 37:1; 40:1.) They are awesome—literally full of awe! And to have an exchange with a "righteous spirit made perfect" who is part of the great cloud of witnesses adds another dimension.

What is the real significance of these complex supernatural experiences? A main benefit is that our prejudices are put on pause, and we can be in a place to receive God's thoughts on a matter on a level that we would not have been able to perceive previously. In such a case, the message God wants us to receive has significant weight, and He wants to make sure we get it. For instance, God put Peter into a trance to deal with his preconceived prejudices against the Gentiles so that Peter could pave the way for the gospel to go beyond the Jews. (See Acts 10.) God was able to bypass Peter's hang-ups. God's "super" got put in front of his "natural," and his mindset was renewed.

These experiences can be very subjective, which is why I recommend that the more subjective the experience, the greater accountability you must have, and the greater a grounding in the Word of God is required. After his experience, Peter got called out by the Jewish believers for eating with the Gentiles. Acts 11:4 (NASB) says that Peter *"explained at length to them in an orderly sequence"* what had happened, including his experiencing the trance. He was being held accountable. Peter also confirmed the message he had received in this encounter by the words of Jesus. In Acts 11:16 (NASB, NASB95), he said, *"And I remembered the word of the Lord...."* Verse 18 (NASB, NASB95) describes the response of everyone listening: *"When they heard this, they quieted down and glorified God."* I love that! There is both great wisdom and power in accountability to others and to the Word of God.

In Zechariah 3:7, God promises, *"If you will walk in My ways, and if you will keep My command, then you shall also judge My house, and likewise have charge of My courts; I will give you places to walk among these who stand here."* I want to conclude with a few guidelines or cautions regarding the ways in which we are to walk in the council room:

1. *Guard against unhealthy familiarity and fascination with personage.* I know highly gifted people who became so overly familiar with these ways that they ended up in hubris. One person started bragging about how he had met so-and-so in heaven, and this person supposedly told him who the writer of the book of Hebrews was. You know what? If the Bible doesn't tell us who wrote the book of Hebrews, I don't think this person has permission to tell us who wrote the book of Hebrews.

2. *Avoid the temptation to worship these experiences or what you encounter there.* Revelation 19:10 tells us that John was tempted to worship angels; the angel's response is advice we should follow: *"Worship God!"*

3. *Stay curious and continue to look and learn during an encounter.* In their respective books, both Daniel and Ezekiel say that they repeatedly looked and watched during their encounters. Daniel was so bold as to not only look but also ask questions. Daniel 7:16 says, *"I came near to one of those who stood by, and asked him the truth of all this. So he told me and made known to me the interpretation of these things."*

4. *Do not be flippant.* I have heard of some people commanding angels. I make an appeal for us to follow the example of Jesus in this matter. Matthew 26:53 (NLT) records the words of Jesus after He was betrayed and as He was being arrested to be crucified: *"Don't you realize that I could ask my Father for thousands of angels to protect us, and he would send them instantly?"* Who is doing the commanding of angels? Not Jesus. He said He would

ask the Father. My point is that Jesus Himself did not walk in a flippant manner with regard to commanding angels. Neither should we.[43]

5. *Be discerning as you encounter the spiritual realm.* Years ago, there was a very popular book from a woman who claimed she had gone to heaven. But the heaven she had actually experienced was only the second heaven, where the principalities and powers dwell and which is a battleground in spiritual warfare, and the truths she was advocating were doctrines of demons. She did not have proper discernment to distinguish between an angelic encounter and its demonic counterfeit.[44]

Supernatural experiences can clearly be complex and intense. In the final two chapters, we will continue to discover how to walk wisely in divine encounters so that we can avoid the traps of the enemy and enjoy the blessings of God as we stand strong in the glorious anointing of the Holy Spirit.

PRAYER TO GROW IN DISCERNING SUPERNATURAL EXPERIENCES

Wonderful Father, in the great name of Jesus, I desire to grow in every area of supernatural encounters for the glory of God. As for me and my house, I want everything that You want for me. If it be heavenly visitations, trances, or standing in the council room of heaven, then that is what I want. If, in the past, I have ever attempted to project myself by self-will or moved in any form of violation to Your laws of the Spirit, forgive me, in Jesus's name. Thank You for the precious encounters that cause us to fall more in love with You. Amen and amen.

---

43. In my book *Angelic Encounters*, I lay out a clear biblical presentation on the issue of not walking in presumption and of the way in which angelic activity is released.
44. To learn more about these subjects, see my books *Angelic Encounters*, *Deliverance from Darkness* (Grand Rapids, MI: Chosen Books, 2010), *The Seer*, and *The Discerner*.

WISDOM, BOUNDARIES, AND SAFEGUARDS FOR YOUR JOURNEY

"Therefore whoever hears these sayings of Mine, and does them, I will liken him to a wise man who built his house on the rock."
—Matthew 7:24

As supernatural encounters become a part of our lives, it is important for us to maintain a solid foundation. That foundation includes a desire for our character to match our gifting. Love must be our aim while, at the same time, we earnestly desire spiritual gifts. We need a house that is built to last against storms that rage, winds that blow, and waves that roar. With this in mind, let me share with you a dream I had that I call "The House That Is Built to Last." I do not give titles to all my dreams, but the Holy Spirit gave me a title for this one.

During a time of rest, I received a very vivid dream that was more apostolic in content and nature. In this revelatory encounter, I was taken to a construction site where the foundation of a house was being prepared. Two angels came and stood at the front of each corner of the property, overseeing the forthcoming construction. The ground was rocky, and the earth was crying out for a deep, strong, firm foundation to be laid, as there had been many shakings and earthquakes in the region over the years.

Very deep trenches were dug, and cement trucks appeared on the scene to pour the foundation. The first layer of cement was poured, and I watched as it set up to dry. Writing in script appeared on the right-hand front of the foundation, stating, "Jesus Christ—the Messiah of the Jew and the Gentile." As I continued to watch, script appeared on the left front, stating, "Apostles and Prophets—Fathers and Mothers of the Ages." This dream was providing instruction, but the overriding atmosphere or emotion was the jealousy of God.

The dream continued into the next phase. Cement trucks pulled up again, and another pouring proceeded as I kept watching in the Spirit. Script appeared again on the second layer of the foundation as it began to set up. On the front corner on the right-hand side, the word "Humility" emerged, and on the left, "Integrity" manifested. The scene repeated a third time, with a phrase surfacing to the top of the freshly poured cement. This time, the script stated to me, "Intimate worship from a pure heart." I was now keenly aware that this was no ordinary house that was about to be built. It was an apostolic house for the glory of God in the end times.

Another cement truck came and unloaded its quick-drying substance. Once again, words appeared: "God's heart for the poor and the desperate." As soon as these words rose to the top, another phrase sprang forth into view: "God's healing presence." The foundation now appeared to be complete as a demonstration of the power of God was established for the foundation of the house.

Suddenly, or so it seemed, I was awakened from out of this detailed dream with a word from the angels that were overseeing the construction of the house. With the presence of the "jealousy of God," I clearly heard, "This is the house that is built to last." I lay in my bed, marveling over the wisdom that permeated this God encounter.

In these days before Christ's return, the Holy Spirit is sending us help to make sure that the foundation of each of our personal lives is strong, secure, and "built to last." This is true, as well, for the corporate dwelling place of God—the church, the body of Christ. Here are five questions to ask ourselves:

1. Is Jesus, the Messiah, the cornerstone of my life?

2. Is my house established upon the revelation, lifestyle, and truths of the apostles and prophets—the fathers and mothers of the faith throughout the ages of the church?

3. Am I maintaining a life of integrity and humility, with a heart filled with pure worship?

4. Am I asking the Lord to restore the ancient foundation of God's heart for the poor and the desperate?

5. Am I seeking the Lord for a greater release of His healing presence to demonstrate His love and mercy?

Since having this dream, I have been consistently asking myself and the Lord these questions and evaluating my life. My life has been full of supernatural encounters, and I need these questions to keep me grounded. So now I ask you the same questions that the "jealousy of God" has been asking me. Is your house built to last? When the winds, rains, and storms that Jesus spoke about come, will your house remain standing? Let us acquire wisdom from the Lord and build our houses so that they will stand firm as a testimony of His greatness! The storms of life will come. Let "The House That Is Built to Last" come forth for the glory of God![45]

Every house that is built to last must also be cared for. This requires wisdom, healthy boundaries, and safeguards. In this chapter, we'll look at three traps and how to avoid them so we can stand strong in the anointing: familiar spirits that imitate; insecurity that can lead to emotional and spiritual bondage; and old wineskins that will not hold the new wine of the Spirit. Let's dive in.

WARNING CONCERNING FAMILIAR SPIRITS[46]

Paul could not have been clearer to Timothy when he said, *"The Spirit explicitly says that in later times some will fall away from the faith, paying attention to deceitful spirits and doctrines of demons"* (1 Timothy 4:1 NASB95). Paul had experienced some breathtaking spiritual encounters, and we see in his letters an attempt to bring some wisdom and healthy boundaries concerning them so that followers of Christ would not be deceived. The Holy Spirit had told Paul *"explicitly"* that some would fall away because they paid attention to deceitful spirits and their teachings.

In my opinion, one of the most sly, deceitful demonic spirits is a familiar spirit. Why? Because it mimics or imitates the Holy Spirit and His work, or it impersonates a loved one, a biblical character, or someone we would normally trust. Familiar spirits attempt to be copycats. What does God think about them? Leviticus 20:27 says, *"A man or a woman who is a medium, or who has familiar spirits, shall surely be put to death; they shall stone them with stones. Their blood shall be upon them."* Whoa. God is not a fan of spirits that appear

---
45. Chapter 12, "Finishing Well," in my book *Living a Supernatural Life* has a full presentation of this content.
46. My book *The Discerner* has even more in-depth teaching on this topic.

to offer one thing when they have a completely different purpose. In the visionary world, not only do we need to discern the difference between the actual and the symbolic, but, more importantly, we must discern the authentic source from the fake source of a supernatural encounter.

My emphasis at the start of this chapter on having a solid foundation was extremely purposeful. Why? Because having a faulty foundation can lead someone—even one who is called and gifted—to deceptive roads that will take them into fantasy trips. God gives gifts from His place of divine calling. But it is our role to prepare our lives to be able to carry the gifts. Faulty foundations in our lives ultimately lead to openings that the god of this world will seek to take advantage of. This may result in a mixture where genuinely gifted people are deceived and begin to receive revelation from more than one source—God *and* the enemy's evil spirits.

I didn't say that these people weren't still receiving from God, the source of genuine giftedness. But when a fracture is present, misconceptions can happen when people handle the anointing. A fracture in the soul that is not healed creates an opening that can lead to deception. And then the person can step into a mixture of fantasy and truth because of their distorted view through a fractured lens.

My dad had a lumberyard and was a master craftsman at working with glass and windows. If a windowpane was clear, then the image on the other side of the window was clear. But if the windowpane had bubbles, wrong curvatures, or was cracked, then the view through the window was distorted. The problem was not the person looking through the window or what appeared to be distorted on the other side of the window. The problem was the defect in the window that was causing the distortion. The clarity of the windowpane, what we look through, makes all the difference.

In the same way, there is no problem with the gift of God. It comes from Him in a pure form that is ready for use. But what we see will not be accurate if we have an unhealed fracture in our souls distorting the truth. Do you know the way that people used to clean glass? They would use newspaper and vinegar. Well, we need to take the newsprint of God's Word and clean the window's "pain." There is pain on our pane, but through the newsprint of the good news of the Word of God, we can get the pain out of the window of our soul. Then we will have clear perception without distortion and be able to recognize familiar spirits or other deceptive tactics of the enemy because we will see things as they are from God's perspective.

This is why it's important to regularly check the lens of our soul. If we need to get our natural eyes checked once a year, shouldn't we check on our spiritual vision at least that often? Sometimes things have gotten fuzzy, and we need an updated prescription for new lenses. Let's all do regular checkups. Yes, keep your physical eyes healthy *and* also have regular checkups with the Holy Spirit so that God can point out distorted perspectives. The Holy Spirit will warn us against familiar spirits or other areas of deception and provide an opportunity for healing from fractures in our foundation so we can perceive correctly.

Now, I am not talking about perfectionism. God uses people who are in the process of growth to bring healing to other people who are in process. Did you catch that? God always uses people in process to bring healing to other people in process, because this is about grace empowerment. But let's also allow the Holy Spirit to do His wonderful work in our lives so we don't have ongoing unhealed fractured places in our windowpanes that, over time, allow distortion to occur.

PRACTICALLY MOVING INTO WHOLENESS[47]

No matter how anointed you are, you have to deal with life. Christian history has far too many highly anointed people who blew up their lives due to unhealed personal issues. Even those who appear to have it all together on stage can be falling apart in private. While God honors brokenness, we don't have to stay broken in areas Jesus died to make whole. Remaining broken in those areas is a trap that undermines your ability to stand strong in the anointing. Don't let God's blessings fall through the cracks! One crack that makes our foundation unstable is insecurity. Here are three basic steps to move from insecurity to wholeness.

STEP 1: FORGIVING

Forgiving ourselves and others is the first step to being set free of emotional and spiritual bondages. We must learn to properly deal with guilt. There are three types of guilt: true, false, and exaggerated. True guilt is what you feel when you've done something wrong, and the Holy Spirit is convicting you of what happened. False guilt happens when the enemy accuses you of something, but it's just not true, yet you experience feelings of guilt. Then there is exaggerated guilt, where there is partial truth to the guilt, but then the false guilt gets blown way out of proportion. Essentially, each of these types of guilt must be dealt with in the same manner: by cleansing through the blood of the Lord Jesus Christ!

Hebrews 9:11–14 (NLT) declares the good news of the finished work of Christ:

> *So Christ has now become the High Priest over all the good things that have come. He has entered that greater, more perfect Tabernacle*

---

47. In my book *The Prophet*, I have an entire chapter on "The Prophet and the Rejection Syndrome," which addresses this topic more completely. I also cover in detail the subject of healing the wounded spirit and other related subjects in my study guide *The Healing Anointing* (Franklin, TN: EN Productions, 2013).

in heaven, which was not made by human hands and is not part of this created world. With his own blood—not the blood of goats and calves—he entered the Most Holy Place once for all time and secured our redemption forever. Under the old system, the blood of goats and bulls and the ashes of a heifer could cleanse people's bodies from ceremonial impurity. Just think how much more **the blood of Christ will purify our consciences from sinful deeds so that we can worship the living God.** *For by the power of the eternal Spirit, Christ offered himself to God as a perfect sacrifice for our sins.*

True guilt, false guilt, and exaggerated guilt all condemn the conscience, and guilt can be removed only by the forgiveness that comes through the blood of Christ. We can actually purify or cleanse our consciences with the blood of Jesus. Leviticus 16:21–22 (NLT) gives us a picture of how that guilt gets removed:

[The high priest] *will lay both of his hands on the [scape]goat's head and confess over it all the wickedness, rebellion, and sins of the people of Israel. In this way, he will transfer the people's sins to the head of the goat. Then a man specially chosen for the task will drive the goat into the wilderness. As the goat goes into the wilderness, it will carry all the people's sins upon itself into a desolate land.*

What a fascinating foreshadowing of what Christ would accomplish on the cross!

When we confess our sins, we are putting them on Christ so He can take them away from us. Psalm 103:12 declares the liberating truth that "*as far as the east is from the west, so far has He removed our transgressions from us.*" Confession is the spiritual key that unlocks forgiveness. For "*if we confess our sins, he is faithful and just and will forgive us our sins and purify us from all unrighteousness*" (1 John 1:9 NIV).

Your conscience can act like flypaper. Whatever is flying around gets stuck to it. Eventually, you have to get rid of it because it's full of dead flies. To get rid of a guilty conscience, you have to put the source of the guilt on the scapegoat and shoo it away. Practically speaking, confess words out of your mouth to Jesus that describe the guilt you are feeling and why. Then ask Him to take it away.

Forgiving yourself and others is an act of the will, so choosing to forgive is the first step toward healing. If you wait to feel like forgiving, you may never forgive. Forgiving—whether you feel forgiveness or not—is a spiritual act that allows your emotions to become healed or sanctified, made whole enough eventually, and come into alignment. But you cannot wait until you're emotionally healed to forgive. Forgiveness is the first step, and it starts with a deliberate choice.

STEP 2: FORGETTING

Unfortunately, there is no spiritual gift called amnesia. I'm not recommending that you live in a fantasy land or spend all your time distracting yourself from your pain, but I do want to say that forgetting is healthy and important. I admit there is a tension between reality and forgetting, so let's look at that for a moment.

Forgetting involves several things. First, you cannot forget what you have not yet given to Jesus. Justice will continue to cry out, "Something wrong happened. Deal with it!" But after you have confessed your sinful deeds and been cleansed by the blood of Jesus, it's time to discard the offense. You may also need to remove a judgmental spirit against other people, erase the scoreboard that shows how many wrongs have been committed against you, and even ignore all the good things you did that got trampled on by others, life's circumstances, or even yourself.

How many times do we have to forgive? Peter asked Jesus this question. I'm sure he thought he was being generous when he offered an answer to his own question: *"Up to seven times?"* (Matthew 18:21). But then Jesus replied, "Oh, it's more like seventy times seven." (See verse 22). So, Peter's thinking, "Praise God, that's 490. I'm at 410 with this one guy who's really a bother. I've got only 80 more to go." But Jesus wasn't giving a legalistic answer. He was saying we need to forgive an indefinite number of times…way more than we want to. I believe He was also showing us that forgiveness is like a yo-yo in that you toss out the offense, and it comes back. You throw it out—you've finally forgiven that person—only to have it return. How many times do you have to do this? The answer may vary according to the person or the situation. But there will come a day that you'll throw out the offence, the string will break, and it will no longer come back. As you continue to persist in forgiveness, a day will come when you actually feel forgiven or that you have finally released the sin.

Philippians 3:13–14 shows us the importance of forgetting. In fact, it was the *"one thing"* Paul said he was doing: *"One thing I do: forgetting what lies behind and reaching forward to what lies ahead, I press on toward the goal for the prize of the upward call of God in Christ Jesus"* (NASB, NASB95). Your pressing forward is significantly limited until you forget what lies behind.

Forgetting is so refreshing, and it's so nonreligious. Forgetting makes three statements:

1. *A statement of vulnerability:* "I haven't arrived." It is extremely refreshing to come across very capable, competent people who have retained their vulnerability and humility, acknowledging that they're still a work in progress.

2. *A statement of realism:* "I forget what is behind." When mistreated or hurt by another, an honest, authentic, real person makes the hard choice to forgive and forget.

3. *A statement of determination:* "I press on." Those who choose not to forget remain tied to the past, the abuse, the immaturity, and

the dysfunction. Those who forgive and forget can move ahead to new, positive areas.

Practically speaking, forgetting...

- Reminds me, as if I need reminding, that I have flaws, just as others do.
- Enables me to be gracious and encouraging, not petty and negative.
- Frees me to live for this moment and tomorrow rather than being anchored to yesterday.

STEP 3: RELEASING

The third step of this process is vital. You must release control of the individual, group, or circumstance and put the situation into God's hands. We each have Abraham-Isaac situations in our lives where we have to yield expectations, unmet desires, and promises back to God. We must relinquish our hopes, fears, hurts, goals, longings, and yearnings, as well as the very person or event involved in the situation.

In the parable Jesus told in response to Peter's question about the number of times we should forgive, He concluded with, *"And the lord of that slave felt compassion and released him and forgave him the debt"* (Matthew 18:27 NASB95). Releasing is a final step to be able to forgive. This releasing may be climaxed in a prayer in which you:

- Give the person or event to God.
- Let go of your expectations, hurts, or pains.
- Renounce emotional dependency.
- Ask the Lord for a blessing upon the situation.

+ Ask God for grace to turn away and walk free from self-condemnation.

By the way, this is a process—typically not just a onetime prayer. Again, emotional healing often comes in layers. Remember the yo-yo that seems to want to come back until the string finally breaks. But if you persist in this process, you will know the truth, and it will set you free. (See John 8:31–32.) *"If the Son makes you free, you shall be free indeed"* (John 8:36).

A PARADIGM SHIFT FOR A NEW WINESKIN

In our search for the wisdom ways of God, setting in place proper boundaries and guardrails for walking through the maze of supernatural encounters, we also need to consider some structural changes. We need to change our minds in at least three areas, in which we go from "lone ranger" to body alignment, from teaching to fathering, and from immature to mature.

This is not just for supernatural encounters. These are God's wisdom ways for every part of our lives. These three elements will help to form a new wineskin that will hold the new wine.

FROM LONE RANGER TO BODY ALIGNMENT

Long gone are the days when we can stand and minister alone. Standing strong in the anointing means standing with others. Again, Isaiah 65:8 declares the truth that *"the new wine is found in the cluster."* There is also safety when you are part of something bigger than yourself. Wolves in the wild strategically look for an animal that is alone, or they will try to separate an animal from its herd, to attack it. We are ones who are sent out as *"lambs among wolves"* (Luke 10:3), so we'd better stay with the pack.

Paul was clear in his teaching that each part of the body is important, and each is a contributing member of the whole body, where there is unity and care. (See 1 Corinthians 12:12–31.) The Greek word translated *"equipping"* in the phrase *"equipping of the saints"* in Ephesians 4:12 means "bringing to a condition of fitness, perfecting." The Hebrew equivalent of this concept is to "make straight, set right,"[48] similar to how chiropractic treatment brings the body into alignment. The body of Christ that is needed to catch the great harvest of souls that is coming must be aligned and united. We really are better together!

FROM TEACHING TO FATHERING

A second adjustment that is needed is to move from teaching to relational fathering. Yes, this is a big one! Jesus taught the multitudes, but He relationally discipled the Twelve. In his letters, Paul addressed Timothy as *"a true son in the faith"* (1 Timothy 1:2). The relationship between Elijah and Elisha is another model for us to follow. Notice Elisha's cry recorded in 2 Kings 2:12 as Elijah was being taken away from him: *"And Elisha saw it, and he cried out, 'My father, my father, the chariot of Israel and its horsemen!'"* (2 Kings 2:12). Elisha cried out… what? *"My father"*—twice. Elijah was not just Elisha's mentor. Elisha saw something greater and honored Elijah as a father.

Paul said to the Corinthian church, *"For even if you had ten thousand others to teach you about Christ, you have only one spiritual father. For I became your father in Christ Jesus when I preached the Good News to you"* (1 Corinthians 4:15 NLT). We have many teachers but not many fathers and mothers. Yet it's time for this to change. We must make a shift from having an orphan spirit to receiving a spirit of adoption where we each become secure in our identity in Christ Jesus, and we grow into the full stature that God intends. Even if we do not have an intimate relationship with a father, mother, grandfather, or

---

48. *Strong's Exhaustive Concordance of the Bible*, G2677, καταρτισμός (*katartismos*), Bible Hub, https://biblehub.com/greek/2677.htm.

grandmother of great stature in the faith, we can always have an intimate relationship with God the Father.

FROM IMMATURE TO MATURE

I'm grateful to Bill Hamon, founder of Christian International Ministries and a modern father of the global prophetic movement, for allowing me to reprint the following, which he calls "The 10 M's for Determining True Ministers."[49] These "10 M's" are a powerful, personal checklist as we consider our own level of maturity. Notice that none of these areas of qualification is about giftedness. They all deal with important issues for the messenger and how they carry the message, which determine our ability to stand strong in the anointing, avoiding the traps and embracing the blessings of the fullness of the Holy Spirit. As you read, take inventory of your own life.

1. Manhood (this applies to women as well):

    + God makes a man before manifesting mighty ministry (Genesis 1:26–27)

    + Conformed to the image of Christ—apart from position, message, or ministry (Romans 8:29)

    + Personality: evaluating person, not performance (Hebrews 2:6, 10)

    + Jesus: growing in maturity for thirty years, ministry for three and a half years: a 10:1 ratio (1 Timothy 2:5)

2. Ministry:

    + No offense to ministry (2 Corinthians 6:3)

---

49. A similar version of this material can be found online. See Bishop Bill Hamon, "Raising God's Standards: 'Ten M's' for Prophetic Leaders by Bishop Bill Hamon," Eagles Nest Ministries, http://eaglesnestministries.org/raising-gods-standards-ten-ms-for-prophetic-leaders-by-bishop-bill-hamon/. Used with permission.

- Power and demonstration (1 Corinthians 2:4–5)
- By their fruits you shall know them—anointing and results (Matthew 7:15–21)
- Prophecies or preaching must be proven, pure, and positive (Deuteronomy 18:20–22)

3. Message:
   - Speak the truth in love; present life-giving truth (Ephesians 4:15)
   - Message is balanced, scriptural, doctrinally sound, and spiritually right (1 Timothy 4:2)
   - God confirms His Word—not person, pride, or reputation (Mark 16:20)

4. Maturity:
   - Attitude right; mature in human relations; heavenly wisdom (James 3:17)
   - Fruit of the Spirit, Christlike character, dependable, steadfast (Galatians 5:22)
   - Not childish (1 Corinthians 13)
   - Biblically knowledgeable and mature; not a novice (Hebrews 5:14; Ephesians 4:14; 1 Timothy 3:6)

5. Marriage:
   - Scripturally in order; manage personal family before God's family (1 Timothy 3:2, 5)
   - Priorities straight: God first, then spouse and family, then ministry (1 Peter 3:1, 7)

- Marriage to exemplify relationship between Christ and His church (Ephesians 5:22–23)

6. Methods:

    - Rigidly righteous, ethical, honest, having integrity, upright (Titus 1:16)

    - Not manipulative or deceptive (Romans 1:18)

    - Good end results do not justify unscriptural methods (Romans 3:7–8)

7. Manners:

    - Unselfish, polite, kind; gentleman or lady; discreet (Titus 1:7; 3:1–2)

    - Proper speech and communication in words and mannerisms (Ephesians 4:29; 5:4)

8. Money:

    - "Not greedy for base gain [craving wealth and resorting to ignoble and dishonest methods of getting it]" (1 Timothy 3:8 AMPC).

    - Love of money and materialism destroys, as may be seen in the lives of Achan, Balaam, and Judas (Luke 12:15; 1 Timothy 6:5, 10, 17)

9. Morality:

    - Virtuous, pure, and proper relationships (1 Corinthians 6:9–18; Colossians 3:5)

    - Biblical sexual purity in attitude and action (Ephesians 5:3; 1 Corinthians 5:11)

- Wrong thoughts with desire to do—without opportunity to act (Matthew 5:28)

10. Motive:

    - To serve or to be seen? Fulfill personal drive or God's desire? (Matthew 6:1)

    - True motivation? To minister or to be a minister? (1 Corinthians 16:15–16)

    - To herald the truth or just be heard by man? (Proverbs 16:2)

    - Motivated by God's love or by lust for power, fame, name? (1 Corinthians 13:1–3)

How I long to be like Christ, and I know this is your desire as well. Let's pray to grow in God's wisdom ways so that *"we all come to such unity in our faith and knowledge of God's Son that we will be mature in the Lord, measuring up to the full and complete standard of Christ"* (Ephesians 4:13 NLT). Amen!

PRAYER TO GROW IN WISDOM WAYS FOR YOUR JOURNEY

Almighty Father, in the wonderful name of Jesus, I continue to ask for Your wisdom, which comes down from above, as it says in James 3:17. I am not looking for the wisdom of man but rather for a supernatural wisdom that includes the divine intelligence of the Holy Spirit and His gifts. Expose any wrong thinking and old structures that are not useful as new wineskins to carry the new wine. Deliver me from any deception of familiar spirits or any hindrance that is in the way of my being a good steward for the new era. I choose to embrace wisdom boundaries that will keep me and others in safe, pleasant places. I declare that I am a part of the body of Christ that is establishing new paradigms for the second apostolic age of the church. Thank You, Holy Spirit, for allowing me to be a part of Your great plans and purposes in this generation. For the glory of God, amen and amen!

12

THE GOAL OF SUPERNATURAL ENCOUNTERS: REVEALING JESUS

> *"At this I fell at his feet to worship him. But he said to me, 'Don't do that! I am a fellow servant with you and with your brothers and sisters who hold to the testimony of Jesus. Worship God! For it is the Spirit of prophecy who bears testimony to Jesus.'"*
> —Revelation 19:10 (NIV)

This final chapter is the most important because it is about the goal of supernatural encounters. However, what I am about to share is not only the goal of supernatural encounters—it should also be the life goal of every disciple of the Lord Jesus Christ. What is that goal? To reveal Jesus and to see Him in all things.

The context of Revelation 19:10, our theme verse for this chapter, is that John the Beloved is on the isle of Patmos in isolation, but he is not alone. While he is in worship on the Lord's Day, he sees the Lord Jesus Christ and also has a dramatic supernatural encounter with angels. The angelic encounter is so glorious that John is actually tempted to enter into worship of the angel until the angel warns him, *"Don't do that! I am a fellow servant with you and with your brothers and sisters who hold to the testimony of Jesus. Worship God! For it is the Spirit of prophecy who bears testimony to Jesus."* This is our testimony: the worship of Jesus. Lord, help us to see through the maze of the beauty of supernatural encounters and to fulfill their ultimate purpose: to see You high and lifted up, with Your glory both filling our temples and filling the earth. (See, for example, Isaiah 6:1; Habakkuk 2:14.)

THREEFOLD CORD OF TRUTH

You've read enough in this book to know that I am not anti-supernatural encounters. Yet I want to be crystal clear about my stance: I am pro-supernatural encounters that lead us into the glorious testimony that Jesus Christ is Lord. How can we ensure that all our supernatural encounters lead us in this direction?

Ecclesiastes 4:12 (NIV) says, *"Though one may be overpowered, two can defend themselves. A cord of three strands is not quickly broken."* I have used this reference many times at wedding ceremonies as it pertains to the covenant of marriage. This verse also applies to business transactions, the formation of proper governmental alliances, and the true value of friendship. In our study of how to stand strong in the anointing, especially when we encounter the supernatural, I find that the principle holds true once again: a three-cord strand of truth needs to be brought together. That threefold cord of truth is as follows: (1) being grounded in the Word of God, (2) being grounded in the precedent of Jewish and church history, and (3) being grounded in contemporary experience.

1. *Grounded in the Word of God.* As the days of our end times unfold, we must make sure that what we believe is grounded in the Word of God, first and foremost! Many people will claim extra special revelation from extra special sources. I say, "Slow down a moment. Do you

know how to test the spirits to see if they are of God? There is no higher authority than the Word of God itself!" We must ground our supernatural encounters in the Word of God—both the *logos*, or the written Word, and the *rhema*, which is either a portion of the Word quickened to us by the Spirit at a specific time for a given need or circumstance, or a word from God spoken prophetically.

2. *Grounded in the precedent of Jewish and church history.* What comes around has already been around. *"There is nothing new under the sun"* (Ecclesiastes 1:9). When evaluating supernatural encounters, after looking to the Scriptures, I search to see if there is precedent in Jewish and church history. This, too, can be an exhaustive and delightful study to venture out on. I remember when I started tackling the controversial subject of trances, and I found multiple accounts of them in Scripture. But perhaps the days of our experiencing trances have faded away to be no more. Well, at least, that's what some people thought.

I discovered many such diverse examples in the lives of the Hebrew prophets and a treasure chest of examples in early church history, such as in the lives of Saint Teresa of Ávila, Saint John of the Cross, and the Christian mystics. As I continued my search, I found many more modern-day examples in the lives of people described by H. A. Baker in his book *Visions Beyond the Veil*. Through these additional resources, I discovered that accounts of spiritual trances are in the Word of God *and* noted throughout Jewish and church history.

3. *Grounded in contemporary experience.* The third part of the three-cord strand of truth in theology and in life is contemporary experience. Since *"Jesus Christ is the same yesterday, today, and forever"* (Hebrews 13:8), we should be able to expect what we see in the Bible to occur in our lives today. I have learned to read biographies of heroes in the faith and gather morsels from their testimonies of supernatural encounters. I have also had the privilege of sitting with godly generals in the faith in a culture of honor, gleaning from their fifty-plus-year narratives. Then

I have my own contemporary experiences that help to comprise this third strand. You can do the same in building your three-cord strand of truth!

Did you know that I still practice this process of employing the three-cord strand to this day? I did this for the topic of dreams, which is why my material in *Dream Language* is so thorough. I followed this process for *The Seer* as well. When that book came out, the Christian Booksellers Association didn't know how to categorize it because there are three hundred Scripture references in it. So, they categorized it under "Bible Studies."

I say all this to encourage you to do your due diligence when it comes to supernatural encounters. Ground them in the Word of God, in Jewish and church history, and in contemporary experiences. This will be a key to standing strong in the anointing, avoiding the traps, and embracing the blessings of the God encounters you have.

CULTIVATING THE FEAR OF THE LORD

Walking in the fear of the Lord is another essential key to operating wisely in divine encounters. John Witherspoon (1723–1794), a noted preacher, president of the College of New Jersey (now Princeton University), and the only clergyman who signed the Declaration of Independence, stated in a sermon, "It is only the fear of God [that] can deliver us from the fear of man."[50] Given Witherspoon's influence, he knew something about the fear of the Lord:

> Some historians believe Witherspoon became the most influential college president in American history, since nine of the

---

50. John Witherspoon, "Ministerial Character and Duty," sermon, Antiquarian Books of Scotland, uploaded by the National Library of Scotland, https://digital.nls.uk/antiquarian-books-of-scotland/archive/115088702?mode=transcription.

fifty-five delegates to the Constitutional Convention were former students of his; also from among his personally-taught Princeton students came three Supreme Court Justices, ten cabinet officers, twelve members of the Continental Congress, twenty-eight United States Senators and forty-nine members of the U. S. House of Representatives.[51]

What is the fear of the Lord? This concept can be misunderstood, so let's see how the Bible defines it. A number of Scriptures help us see what it looks like:

- *"To fear the L*ORD *is to hate evil; I hate pride and arrogance, evil behavior and perverse speech"* (Proverbs 8:13 NIV).

- *"The fear of the Lord—that is wisdom, and to shun evil is understanding"* (Job 28:28 NIV).

- *"The fear of the L*ORD *is the beginning of wisdom; all who follow his precepts have good understanding"* (Psalm 111:10 NIV).

- *"The fear of the L*ORD *is the beginning of wisdom, and knowledge of the Holy One is understanding"* (Proverbs 9:10 NIV).

- *"The fear of the L*ORD *is the beginning of knowledge, but fools despise wisdom and instruction"* (Proverbs 1:7 NIV).

A concise, clear definition of the fear of the Lord that takes all this into account is "to love what God loves and to hate what God hates." I believe there are two ways you can cultivate the fear of the Lord: (1) obey His commands and turn away from evil, and (2) take action by asking for and seeking the wisdom of God for yourself. Let's look at both of these ways.

---

51. Bill Potter, "John Witherspoon Preaches on 'The Dominion of Providence', July 31, 1776," Landmark Events, July 31, 2017, https://landmarkevents.org/john-witherspoon-preaches-on-the-dominion-of-providence-1776/.

1. OBEY GOD'S COMMANDS AND TURN AWAY FROM EVIL

Deuteronomy 6:1–2 (NLT) records this strong exhortation from Moses to the people of Israel:

> *These are the commands, decrees, and regulations that the LORD your God commanded me to teach you. You must obey them in the land you are about to enter and occupy, and you and your children and grandchildren must fear the LORD your God as long as you live. If you obey all his decrees and commands, you will enjoy a long life.*

What an amazing promise comes from obedience through the fear of the Lord: enjoying a long life. A necessary part of obedience is to turn away from, or to "shun," evil. This is what God said of Job when He spoke directly about him to Satan:

> *Then the LORD said to Satan, "Have you considered My servant Job, that there is none like him on the earth, a blameless and upright man, one who fears God and shuns evil? And still he holds fast to his integrity, although you incited Me against him, to destroy him without cause."* (Job 2:3)

God also called out the fear of the Lord in the life of Abraham. Abraham's complete obedience to the Lord's very difficult command demonstrated that he feared the Lord. Genesis 22:10–12 says:

> *And Abraham stretched out his hand and took the knife to slay his son. But the Angel of the LORD called to him from heaven and said, "Abraham, Abraham!" So he said, "Here I am." And He said, "Do not lay your hand on the lad, or do anything to him; for now I know that you fear God, since you have not withheld your son, your only son, from Me."*

2. TAKE ACTION BY ASKING FOR AND SEEKING THE WISDOM OF GOD

Proverbs 2:1–5 (NIV) says:

> *My son, if you accept my words and store up my commands within you, turning your ear to wisdom and applying your heart to understanding—indeed, if you call out for insight and cry aloud for understanding, and if you look for it as for silver and search for it as for hidden treasure, then you will understand the fear of the LORD and find the knowledge of God.*

Look at all the actions that lead to the fear of the Lord through obedience to God's commands: turning, applying, calling out, crying aloud, looking, and searching. There is no room for passivity at all! This is how you cultivate the fear of the Lord. The effort is not easy or popular, but it is the beginning of wisdom, and it is how we find the knowledge of God.

Here are twelve practical benefits of the fear of the Lord for your life, with some representative verses:

1. Instruction and direction from the Lord (Psalm 25:12)
2. Being watched over by the Lord (Psalm 33:18)
3. Angelic protection and deliverance (Psalm 34:7)
4. Protection for you and your children (Proverbs 14:26; 19:23, various translations)
5. Provision (Psalm 34:9)
6. Long life (Psalm 34:11–14; Proverbs 10:27)
7. Compassion from the Lord (Psalm 103:13)
8. Love of the Lord; righteousness for your grandchildren (Psalm 103:17, various translations)

9. Blessing (Psalm 115:13)

10. Wealth and honor (Proverbs 22:4)

11. Praise (Proverbs 31:30)

12. Friendship with God (Psalm 25:14 NLT, ESV)

At the end of the day, there isn't a whole lot you're going to take with you when you die. But there's one thing that will remain forever: friendship with God. And that is what the fear of the Lord will allow you to have. Jesus is the ultimate reward of any supernatural encounter, and the fear of the Lord draws us into a closer relationship with Him.

A LIFE OF INTIMATE WORSHIP FROM A PURE HEART

Very few activities reveal Jesus like when we focus on Him in worship. This is what happened to John. John the Beloved was in exile on the Isle of Patmos, but that did not deter his time of worship on the Lord's Day. No matter his life circumstances, John found himself in adoration of the majesty of the risen Christ. In this place of worship, he was given a divine supernatural encounter that changed his life and the life of every born-again believer. The culminating words, as recorded in Revelation 1:17, state, *"And when I saw Him, I fell at His feet as dead. But He laid His right hand on me, saying to me, 'Do not be afraid; I am the First and the Last.'"* I think this is one of the most stunning supernatural encounters recorded in the entire Bible. John the Beloved sees the Messiah again.

In my book *The Lifestyle of a Prophet,* I use three character sketches to depict different aspects of the prophet's lifestyle. I chose John the Beloved to represent the lifestyle of intimacy. This apostle, this disciple, this ordinary person lived an extraordinary life. But, as an aged man, John was exiled in solitude on Patmos. He seems to have had nothing left in his life. He had been abandoned by men—but not by God. Not at all! God—and His brilliant presence—was now his constant companion. When Jesus is your best friend, others may depart, but He never leaves you or forsakes you. (See Hebrews 13:5.) He is only one act of worship away.

We often think that standing strong in the anointing is about operating in more gifts, learning how to use them strategically for more fruit, and making sure we develop our character to carry the anointing. Yes, these aspects are important, and there are other little keys that open big doors in the supernatural. But the big key that unlocks every door is a life of worship from a pure heart.

As you worship God, Someone—the Great Someone—will inhabit your praises (see Psalm 22:3 KJV), and the Holy Spirit's presence will be poured out. Do you want to become a true messenger of the Lord, with fire burning in your bones? Then have the Man of Fire dwelling in your heart. Worship God passionately. Surrender to Jesus and worship Him! Ascend the hill of the Lord with clean hands and a pure heart. (See Psalm 24:3–6.)

KEY LESSONS ON SEEING JESUS ONLY

I pondered, prayed, and sought God about what closing thoughts to share with you on this most wonderful and unusual topic of supernatural encounters. The Lord led me to Matthew 17:1–8:

Now after six days Jesus took Peter, James, and John his brother, led them up on a high mountain by themselves; and He was transfigured before them. His face shone like the sun, and His clothes became as white as the light. And behold, Moses and Elijah appeared to them, talking with Him. Then Peter answered and said to Jesus, "Lord, it is good for us to be here; if You wish, let us make here three tabernacles: one for You, one for Moses, and one for Elijah." While he was still speaking, behold, a bright cloud overshadowed them; and

> *suddenly a voice came out of the cloud, saying, "This is My beloved Son, in whom I am well pleased. Hear Him!" And when the disciples heard it, they fell on their faces and were greatly afraid. But Jesus came and touched them and said, "Arise, and do not be afraid." When they had lifted up their eyes, they saw no one but Jesus only.*

Jesus takes His inner circle of disciples alone with Him to a high place. He is transfigured, and His face shines like the sun, and His clothes become radiant. Even Moses and Elijah appear before the disciples and converse with Jesus. Peter, in his zeal, wants to make a memorial out of the moment. That is the tendency of us humans. Then the overshadowing presence of God interrupts the supernatural encounter with a strong word: *"But while Peter was still speaking, a bright radiant cloud spread over them, enveloping them all. And God's voice suddenly spoke from the cloud, saying, 'This is my dearly loved Son, the constant focus of my delight. Listen to him!'"* (Matthew 17:5 TPT).

The words *"This is my dearly loved Son"* interrupt Peter's bright idea of making three tabernacles—of building a monument or memorial out of the moment. God the Father and His jealousy break through the whole drama and give a word for us today: *"This is My beloved Son.... Hear Him!"* (Matthew 17:5). The disciples' response is where I want to bring us as we close out these wisdom ways of God regarding supernatural encounters: they fell on their faces in the fear of the Lord, and holy perspective was granted them! They lifted their eyes, and they saw only Jesus.

Did Moses and Elijah just leave? We don't know. The Bible does not say. But the Holy Scriptures report, *"When they had lifted up their eyes, they saw no one but Jesus only"* (verse 8). Did Moses and Elijah fade in the background in comparison? Could be. We don't know if Moses the lawgiver and Elijah the prophet departed, but this is what we do know: Jesus became the center of it all. The fear of the Lord was manifest, and the disciples saw no one but Jesus alone. Selah: pause and reflect on that.

There is one more example of seeing Jesus only that I want to share from church history. In the late 1800s, a woman of prayer and a pioneer of the presence of God named Martha Wing Robinson established the Zion Faith Homes in Zion, Illinois. This simple house-church ministry came into being on the heels of the downfall of the infamous work of Alexander Dowie, who moved profoundly in the working of miracles and gifts of healing with a vision to establish a model city of God on the earth. Dowie cast a large shadow for kingdom purposes that was short-lived.

I have visited Zion, Illinois, and I have studied some of Alexander Dowie's history, which led me to then study Martha Wing Robinson. I found that in the aftermath of some of the fallout that happened, out of the disillusionment that occurred, out of this power gift ministry with Alexander Dowie came a lesser-known ministry that was used to re-center the people of God on the Giver, not just His gifts. Zion Faith Homes exists to this day.

While visiting the Zion Faith Homes, I picked up a copy of a letter from John G. Lake to Elder Brooks of Zion Homes, and Elder Brooks's wisdom-filled reply, which was penned in 1916. The lessons included in these letters were stunning then, and they are perhaps even more stunning today.

John G. Lake was born in Canada and raised in the US. God sent him to South Africa, where he saw an unparalleled release of miracles for about five years. He returned to the US and established a ministry in Spokane, Washington, that saw thousands of miracles. Lake's ministry was amazing, but he hit a time where the gifts of God seemed to dissipate. So he wrote to his friend Elder Brooks.

The letter transparently tells of Lake's own success in power ministry and then how the satisfaction and results began to wane. He was pondering what he needed to do to step back into what he had known. Elder Brooks responded with deep wisdom:

Oh, my Brother John, I once looked for power—wanted equipment; sought usefulness—saw gifts in the distance—knew that dominion was somewhere in the future, but glory to God! One by one these faded, and as they faded, there was a form—a figure emerged from the shadows which became clearer and more distinct as these things faded. When they had passed, I saw "Jesus only."

I am grateful for the permission I received from Zion Faith Homes to share these letters in full.[52] When I read the letters and visited both ministries in Zion, Illinois, and Spokane, Washington, I could not help but think of what I had seen in the account in Matthew 17:1–8, where the disciples, too, saw Jesus only. At the time of the release of this book, I am celebrating fifty years in full-time vocational ministry. For the last several years, this international ministry of prayer, the prophetic, and the presence of God has been called God Encounters Ministries—a ministry to the nations.

While composing this manuscript, I had one of the most dramatic supernatural encounters of my life in the form of a trance. I was standing on a mountaintop with a staff in my hand, dialoguing with a meek prophet named Moses. We were discussing the coming days where the fear of the Lord would be restored to God's people, and signs and wonders would be poured out. It appeared that we stood before hundreds of thousands of people, and the level of authority had greatly increased. As we conversed, a warning was issued: "Do not stretch out the rod of your tongue against God's people in anger. Let kindness rule."

As I came out of this trance state, I felt the stunning presence of the Holy Spirit all over me and an overwhelming awareness that we must keep Jesus the central focus of everything we do. Oh, how I love Jesus because He first loved me!

---

52. You won't find copies of these letters in very many places, but you can read them in the study guide that corresponds to this book, "Understanding Supernatural Encounters Study Guide," which you can find in the online store at GodEncounters.com.

I am grateful for the precious anointing of the Spirit that has kept my ministry well-oiled these fifty years. I have seen signs and wonders and have experienced more than my fair share of supernatural encounters. But as I cross the fifty-year mark of vocational ministry, what stands out most to me is not the anointing to minister but the Anointed One who has stood by my side. Standing strong in the anointing is rooted in the revelation that Jesus Himself is the true blessing of any supernatural encounter.

Please pray with me as a closing declaration of your heart's desire:

PRAYER TO FOCUS ON THE ULTIMATE GOAL

Holy Father, in the magnificent name of Jesus Christ, in my pursuit of supernatural encounters, I want to be like one of the three disciples on the Mount of Transfiguration. When all the superstars fade away, I want to see Jesus only. I want to hear and obey the loveliness of His divine whisper. Help me to cultivate the fear of the Lord, which is the beginning of wisdom. Help me to cherish the three-cord strand of truth in being grounded in the Word of God, in the precedents of Jewish and church history, and in the contemporary experience of the Holy Spirit today. I want what You want! I want to be a modern-day John, the beloved disciple of the Lord Jesus Christ, who lays his head upon the chest of the Messiah. Let that intimacy with God be the foundation for my understanding of supernatural encounters. Help me to keep Jesus the center of it all! For the glory of God, amen and amen!

ABOUT THE AUTHOR

James W. Goll is the founder of God Encounters Ministries and is an international best-selling author, an adviser to leaders and ministries, a vocal recording artist, and a member of ASCAP. He is also the founder of Worship City Alliance and Global Prayer Storm and the cofounder of Women on the Frontlines. James is a member of Harvest International Ministries, the Apostolic Council of Prophetic Elders, and the Global Roundtable of Apostles. He serves as an instructor for the International School of Ministry (ISOM), Wagner University (WU), and Christian Leadership University (CLU).

After pastoring in the Midwest United States, James was thrust into the role of an international equipper and trainer. He has traveled to more than fifty nations, sharing the love of Jesus and imparting the power of intercession, prophetic ministry, and life in the Spirit. His desire is to see the body of Christ become the house of prayer for all nations and to see Jesus Christ receive the rewards of His sufferings.

James has recorded numerous classes with corresponding curriculum kits, and he also offers a yearlong mentoring program available globally at mentoringwithjames.com. He is the author of more than fifty books, including *The Seer, The Discerner, The Feeler, Passionate Pursuit, Dream Language, Praying with God's Heart,* and *The Mystery of Israel and the Middle East.*

James was married to Michal Ann for thirty-two years before her graduation to heaven in the fall of 2008. He has four married children and a growing number of grandchildren. He makes his home in Franklin, Tennessee.

For More Information:

James W. Goll
God Encounters Ministries ✦ P.O. Box 1653 ✦ Franklin, TN 37065
Phone: 1-877-200-1604

Websites:

godencounters.com
mentoringwithjames.com/GEM
globalprayerstorm.com

E-mail:

info@godencounters.com ✦ linktr.ee/GodEncounters

Social Media:

Facebook, Instagram, YouTube, Rumble, ISN, GEM Media, XP Media, iTunes

www.ingramcontent.com/pod-product-compliance
Lightning Source LLC
Chambersburg PA
CBHW070538090426
42735CB00013B/3014